Outing the Bible

Outing the Bible

Queer Folks, God, Jesus, and the Christian Scriptures

Rev. Dr. Nancy Wilson

LifeJourney
PRESS

Grateful acknowledgment is made for permission to quote from the following:

Scripture quotations are from the New Revised Standard Version of the Bible, copyright ©1989 by the Division of Christian Education of the National Council of the Churches of Christ in the U.S.A. Used by permission. All rights reserved.

Excerpts from the ANCHOR BIBLE DICTIONARY by David Noel Freedman, Editor. Copyright © 1992 by Doubleday, a division of Bantam Doubleday Dell Publishing Group, Inc. Used by permission of Doubleday, a division of Bantam Doubleday Dell Publishing Group, Inc.

Published in Indianapolis, Indiana, by LifeJourney Press, LifeJourneyPress.cc. Printed in the United States of America.

Editing by Grant E. Mabie.
Book design and layout by David W. Squire.
Editorial support by Keith Phillips and Johnna VanHoose Dinse.

For other products from LifeJourney Press, visit www.LifeJourneyPress.cc.

For information contact:
The Universal Fellowship of the Metropolitan Community Churches
PO Box 50488
Sarasota, Florida 34232 USA
info@MCCchurch.net
Telephone (310) 360-8640 Fax: (310) 388-1252

To Paula, for a wonderful life of love and surprises,
and for listening to all my stories . . .

Set me as a seal upon your heart,

as a seal upon your arm;

for love is strong as death,

passion fierce as the grave.

Its flashes are flashes of fire,

a raging flame.

Many waters cannot quench love,

neither can floods drown it.

If one offered for love

all the wealth of her house,

it would be utterly scorned.

SONG OF SOLOMON 8:6–7

Special Contributors

The following generous people participated in a crowdfunding campaign that made publication of these two new books possible.

Because of their generosity, many people across the globe will find a spiritual home in MCC and a message of spiritual hope in the Bible. They have given the gift of spiritual life!

Angela and Irma Bauer-Levesque
Patricia A. Beaver and
   Estella M. Thomas
Toby Bishop and Rev. Kevin Downer
Rev. Houston Burnside Jr.
Gilbert Carrasco and Isai DeLaO
Rev. Marian Cavagnaro
Skip Chasey
Beverly Cotton
Rev. Dee and Judy Dale
Dr. Gail Evans, in memory of
   Rev. Jean R. Hart
Don Ferrell and Ronn Valent
Rev. Darlene Garner and
   Rev. Candy Holmes
Lea A. Harthcock
Julie Krueger
Benjamin N. Lamb
Connie Meadows and
   Haviland Houston
Lee Melvin and Carl Williams
Rev. Vickie Miller and Carol Lidey
Carole L. Murrey
Rev. Elijah C. Nealy

Rev. Jane Nelson and Gay Fritzemeier
Sherrill Parmley
Rev. Troy D. Perry and
   Mr. Phillip Ray De Blieck
Rev. Dr. Keith J. Phillips
Robert W. Pope and
   Lawrence Konrad
Rev. Dusty Pruitt and
   Ms. Joanne Rhodes
Deacon Dar Purugganan
Gail Rissler
Rev. Dr. Joan Saniuk and
   Sharilyn Steketee
Rick Sherwin
Toni L. Smith
David F. Sorey and
   Donald L. Johnson
David Squire and David Wene
E. T. Thomas and Pat Beaver
Rev. Donna Twardowski and
   Marilyn A. Kane
Rev. Robin White and
   Chp. Barry Christensen
Byron Yaple

Contents

Acknowledgments ix

1 • Queer Times—Queer Hermeneutics 1

2 • A Lesbian Hermeneutic Of Suspicion 31

3 • Detoxing the "Texts Of Terror". 49

4 • Outing the Sodomite 67

5 • Outing the Bible: Our Queer Texts 75

6 • Jesus Was a Eunuch—And a Lover 95

7 • Same-Sex Relationships in the Bible 113

8 • Angels at the Table 139

Appendix: The Roll Call of Eunuchs 163

Notes 169

Subject Index. 177

Scripture Index 181

Acknowledgments

In some ways, writing a book is a very solitary thing. In many other ways, though, if you are the pastor of a church, it is not! This book originated in the context of pastoring MCC Los Angeles. Rev. Evelyn Kinser worked with me on the idea of moving from the "defense" to the "offense" in treating the subject of homosexuality in the Bible, which evolved, in the changing political vocabulary of our community, to "Outing the Bible." Evelyn was a constant source of encouragement and challenge to me.

Through moving many times, earthquakes, mortgage woes, and untold grief and loss, I learned from the members, friends, staff, and board of MCC Los Angeles the truth of Psalm 46:

> *God is our refuge and strength, a very present help in trouble.*
> *Therefore we will not fear, though the earth should change,*
> *though the mountains shake in the heart of the sea.*

Thanks to the members of my home church, Church of the Trinity MCC in Sarasota, Florida.

Special thanks to those who assisted in the making of this book: Bless you, Sandy Williams, for trips to the library. Thanks to Linda Brenner-Beckstead for all your help, and to Ann Craig for your encouragement and editing.

This book would not have happened without Fr. Malcolm Boyd. When we were doing a "gig" together in San Francisco, Malcolm told me I had to write this book. You are my fairy godfather!

Thank you, Rev. Troy Perry, for starting MCC; for seeing my potential in those early days; for being an incredibly openhearted, open-minded leader; for being willing to be the prophet of God. Thanks to the MCC Elders—Rev. Darlene Garner, Rev. Mona West, Rev. Lillie Brock, Rev.

Ken Martin, and Rev. Hector Gutierrez—for your partnership in MCC's ministry; and thanks to all who have served MCC as Elders. Thanks to Bishop Yvette Flunder whose partnership is giving birth to whole new possibilities for radical inclusion. And, to Barb Crabtree for saying yes to being our Director of Operations.

Thanks to: Dr. Dusty Pruitt, who offered friendship and support when I so much needed it years ago; and colleagues Rabbi Denise Eger and Rev. Dan Smith for your support and encouragement. Thank you Jean Gralley, artist and friend, especially for my first love letters! Thanks to Rev. Pat Bumgardner, friend and colleague in doing justice.

Thanks to my very diverse family. Thank you, Lori Dick, for wisdom, friendship, and quiet presence. Thanks to: Ravi Verma, my spiritual brother, friend, ally; Terri, Dyan and Hannah Ullman-Levine, for safety and home and friendship; my mother, Barbara Wilson, for your encouragement and love; brother Mark; the Chase clan; my other Mom, Marian Schoenwether; and Paula, to whom this book is dedicated.

I want to remember some of my heavenly friends, in addition to the ones who come up in the stories that follow: Vicki Goldish, I still miss you; Rev. Sandy Taylor; Rev. Jim Harris; Dr. Gary McClelland; Edith Perry; Norm Mason; Rev. Jean White; Rev. Jean Hart; and hundreds of others. Dr. John Boswell, whose brilliance can never be replaced—what a model of courageous gay scholarship! Thank you Rev. Danny Mahoney, assistant pastor extraordinaire, who on your deathbed told me to finish the book. Thanks to Patrick, who stuck around only long enough to take care of Danny. Thank you, God, finally, for my dear father Ralph, whose laughter, love, and playfulness are such a blessed memory, and for my brother Dave, also gone too soon.

Thank you, finally, to all the people of Metropolitan Community Churches worldwide for your courage and faithfulness.

1 • Queer Times—Queer Hermeneutics

We queer folk have literally been terrorized by a homophobic world and a church that uses the Bible as a weapon. Christian conservatives are combining fundamentalist use of the Bible with right-wing politics in the United States and all across the world to implement their idea of Christian domination. More often than not, lesbian, gay, bisexual, and transgender concerns are used as leverage to further their campaigns.

Today, we are all beginning to feel what it means to be in the third millennium. Dramatic leaps in technological capacity and social networking amaze us. The Arab "Spring," Occupy Wall Street, and ongoing wars across the globe collide and entwine with human need and human greed. Earthquakes, wildfires, tsunamis, hurricanes, and floods have taken sobering tolls. We are either in the throes of the end or the birth pangs of a new beginning.

In the midst of this, I like to think of us as queer millennialists with an alternative apocalyptic world view.

My use of the word *millennial* is both serious and playful. Judaism and Christianity have *millennial* expressions of eschatology; that is, thinking about the end times—how the world will end, how God will wrap it all up. The actual word millennium comes from the root *mil*, which means thousand, as in "a thousand years." In Jewish and Christian writings there is the promise of an *interregnum*—an in-between time that may last literally for 1,000 years or for some symbolic amount of time. Rabbis, church fathers, church reformers, and 19th- and 20th-century American religious sectarian leaders have debated for more than two millennia about the details. There are those who believe it will happen before Christ returns or the Messiah comes; others believe it will happen after Christ returns.

Sometimes this imagined time period is called the "eighth day of creation." It is expected be marked by any number of things: the destruction of evil, the creation of a new heaven and earth, and the enjoyment on earth of heavenly bliss. Some prophets predict the return of the *ten lost tribes,* while others describe it as the gathering together of *people and tribes.* Millennial fantasies have included predictions of unprecedented earthly fertility, peace, and harmony not only among humans but among animals. Some have imagined endless sumptuous dining and even uninterrupted enjoyment of nuptial bliss! But there is also a downside to the millennial vision: a prediction of Armageddon, the world rule of the anti-Christ, suffering, wars and *rumors* of wars. And, of course, there are debates about whether such suffering will follow or precede an idyllic millennium.

Narrow, literal views of the millennium have characterized some of the more bizarre cults and some particularly negative, exclusionary Protestant sects. On the other hand, a lot of the proliferating New Age philosophies and theologies also abound with quasi-millennialist visions such as the end of the Mayan calendar and the predictions of Nostradamus.

When I use the word millennialist, I am not choosing among several traditional, fixed views of the "end times." I simply want to understand the human longing for "a new heaven on earth;" the persistence of the vision of the "peaceable kingdom" in the midst of contemporary planetary crisis; and a little bit of what Jesus meant by "the kingdom is among you" and his parables that compel us to wait expectantly for the coming of the kingdom.

This queerness of the now and the not yet is a familiar place for lesbian, gay, bisexual, and transgender folks. Our movement blossomed at the end of the second millennium. Judy Grahn offers a wonderful metaphor for this gay and lesbian millennial surge:

> Purple book jackets appeared on books and dictionaries produced by gay poets and writers of both sexes, and purple T-shirts announced gay slogans of affirmation from diverse groups of people from all over the country. As though some mysterious hand had planted bulbs all over the land, we lavender folk sprang up spontaneously flowering in the color we had learned as an identifying mark of our culture when it was subterranean and a secret. Black history month in the United States is February, the shortest month of the year, and gays and lesbians get only the last decade[s] of a whole millennium. It figures.[1]

What about the possibility of a queer millennium? Does that sound too greedy? A queer interregnum, a truly in-between time. A *time-out* for the planet! After all, we queer folks are the quintessential *in-between* folks. Judy Grahn, Mark Thompson, and many others have been documenting the "in-between" gay and lesbian culture and sensibility for decades.

While there is a growing acceptance of queer folk—and Lutheran, Presbyterian, and Episcopal denominations drop prohibitions from their church policies—there is an increasing moral and religious toxicity in many religions, called *fundamentalism*. Fundamentalists accuse those traditions that include women and sexual minorities of rejecting morals, values, and religion. Their absolutes provide clear enemies. Fundamentalism is a kind of collective obsessive thinking, like tunnel vision, and it can function much like an addiction. We stand at a point when right-wing politics cloaked in Christian fundamentalism are being unmasked in the United States, but fundamentalist evangelists are increasingly exporting homophobia and promoting legislative strategies to isolate, imprison, persecute, and execute LGBT people throughout the world.

Into this millennialist moment in history, queer people bring queer hermeneutics to the Bible—a queer interpretation. We stand on the shoulders of people in the African Diaspora, whose hermeneutic of freedom and justice transformed an empire built on slavery and continues to challenge race-based oppression. We stand on the shoulders of feminist, womanist, and mujerista theologians whose heremeutic of suspicion broke open the study of ancient texts.

When we bring a hermeneutic of queer love to the text, we are looking for our own tribal stories of community, ecstasy, and the awkward spaces between and within genders.

We bring a ridiculous faith woven on the loom of our bodies, whose warp is sexual ecstasy and woof is community in an era of HIV/AIDS.

We bring an outrageous belief that Christians have the capacity to live out the core values of the faith: love of God and love of neighbors. We believe people can let go of homophobia and the persecution of queer people in the name of a loving God.

We bring the untenable tenet that Jesus loved the queers of his day and died for us all.

If we are to use a queer hermeneutic to understand the Bible, we need to think about what it means to be queer today. What does it mean to be a gay or lesbian or bisexual or transgender person in the tumult of the now and not yet?

The poet Judy Grahn first spoke powerfully to me about an anthropology or sociology of what she calls *transpeople* (a broad category including gay men, lesbians, transvestites, and transsexuals). For a long time, I have believed that *theological anthropology* (in the old days, this was called the "doctrine of man") was the church's major problem in acceptance of gays and lesbians. Are gay men, lesbians, and trans people a *lobby* for a certain kind of behavior that we want the church to legitimize, or are we a *kind of people?*

And if we are a kind of people, just what kind are we? Michael Cartwright[2] has traced the way 19th- and 20th-century African-American writers, historians, sociologists, and theologians have struggled with questions about black identity. They had to overcome the poisonous pedagogy of the white Christian slaveholders who applied such a critical interpretation to Genesis 9:20–27 and 10:6–11, the story of Ham, in a racist way. Blacks also had to ask the question, "For what reason did God create us? Why did God deliver us from slavery?" Underneath was the question "And why didn't God do it sooner?" or "Why did God let slavery happen at all?"

I spent many years as the pastor of a multicultural church in Los Angeles. I recall the painful voice on the other end of the phone of a black gay man telling me that his lover, HIV-positive and addicted to drugs, had spent the better part of the morning crying out, "Why does God hate us?" He meant African-Americans, that particular *us*. Does our racial or sexual identity have purpose? Does it have meaning? Does our collective suffering or redemption mean anything?

It is relatively new for gays and lesbians to ask deep theological questions. The "love that dare not speak its name" did not dare to theologize much about itself—or even to philosophize much—until recent decades. There is still a risk when we ask such questions. The *problem* with religions that personalize God (like Christianity) is that it then seems logical to personalize disaster or triumph, which results in unbearable guilt, self-aggrandizement, or deep cynicism.

When conservatives blame terrorism, hurricanes, or earthquakes on gay people, they are personalizing disasters in a way that sets human beings up for more mass hysteria and persecution.

In theological circles, understanding how evil and oppression can exist in a world created by God, who is good, is a problem called *theodicy*. Of course, among queer people, who have been told we are evil, we know the personalization of evil can be very destructive.

As a lesbian pastor in the gay, lesbian, bisexual, and transgender community, I have had hundreds of conversations with people agonizing about whether God truly created *us* as we are. And, if so, could God love us; if so, why is there so much suffering, pain, and homophobia? The truth is, I'm not sure I ever really stopped long enough in the early frenetic, even dangerous days to ask those questions myself. I do, however, remember asking these questions to church leaders one night in a restaurant in Vancouver, British Columbia: "Why does the Church hate us? Where does homophobia come from?"

The occasion was a "top-secret" meeting between the leaders of the National Council of Churches of Christ (NCC) in the United States and the Universal Fellowship of Metropolitan Community Churches (MCC) in the summer of 1983.[3] Tensions within the NCC had been mounting over the issue of MCC's application for membership.[4] The Eastern Orthodox churches had issued a statement to the press in the spring, indicating that, if MCC were ever declared *eligible* for membership by the governing board, they would leave the council. But, in fact, the membership committee of the Council (which included an Orthodox member) had unanimously voted in March 1982 that we met all five criteria for membership, and a vote by the council to ratify that judgment had already been postponed for a year and a half.

Meanwhile, MCC leaders and most of the Council were unaware that the president, Bishop James Armstrong, was experiencing a deep emotional crisis that would result in his surprise resignation, surrounded by scandal and rumor, in November 1983. These were the early Reagan years. Ronald Reagan and his administration had no use for the National Council of Churches and its liberal reputation.

In fact, it was on the heels of the Reagan election that both *Reader's Digest* and *60 Minutes* did very biased and damaging exposés on the political activities of the NCC and the World Council of Churches (WCC). This exposure was a major source of political and financial anxiety for the council. So it was with some dismay that the leadership of the NCC also found itself having to deal with an application for membership from a controversial denomination serving a less-than-acceptable minority: homosexuals!

I had admired James Armstrong since my college antiwar activism days. He had *been there*. He was well known for negotiating with the American Indian Movement (AIM) in the early Seventies during the siege at Wounded Knee. He was a classic liberal-activist churchman. I knew gay people who knew him and had worked for him. When he had treated MCC so very coolly in the early days of our application process, I felt disappointed. He knew better, I thought. Where was the courageous moral leadership that we needed at this time?

So when a leader of a major U.S. denomination called me at my home one late spring morning, proposing a top-level, hush-hush meeting with Rev. Troy Perry and myself, I was open and enthusiastic. At last, we had a chance to talk face to face with Armstrong, Dr. Claire Randall (general secretary of the NCC and an extraordinary churchwoman), and the leaders of four of the most powerful and traditionally more liberal denominations.

Meanwhile, all was not well at our headquarters in Los Angeles. At the time, I worked full time for the Fellowship as Clerk of the Board of Elders. In late May, we had learned of the tragic death of Reverend Perry's partner, Greg Cutts. Greg was in the process of emigrating from Canada, after a two-year struggle. Life had been very stressful for Troy and Greg as they tried to manage a long-distance relationship. Both of them were very happy about Greg's impending move. But over the Victoria Day weekend, Greg died in his sleep. In the chaotic weeks that followed, I informed the NCC of Greg's death and told them that we would have to postpone our meeting.

As it happened, all of them would be in Vancouver in July 1983 for the WCC General Assembly. Our finances at the time were dismal, but NCC leaders managed to arrange funding for airfare for one of us to Vancouver, and Troy and I went to meet them "off campus" in a nearby restaurant.

I was worried about Troy and wondered whether or not he should even go to this meeting. But Armstrong had initially talked to him about it, and Troy was curious, I think. To make things more complicated, Greg had died in Vancouver. When we attended the meeting in July, it had only been one month since Troy had been there for Greg's funeral.

We were very cordially greeted in the restaurant. After some small talk, one of the denominational leaders, Arie Brower of the Reformed

Church in America, said softly to Troy, "We are sorry to hear about your recent loss." The Hallmark-greeting-card phrasing seemed awkward but well intentioned. And I was grateful that someone had been willing to acknowledge publicly that Troy's beloved partner had died.

What happened then was a classic case study of the relationship of Metropolitan Community Churches to the NCC. Troy misunderstood the offer of condolences. What he did not know is that people in the liberal middle-class-dominated world of ecumenical politics and etiquette say things like that to put *to rest* a certain matter, not to open it up. The people in that room, though they had known each other for years, knew little, if anything, about each other's personal lives. That became all too evident when Armstrong later resigned. But Troy mistakenly thought he was in a safe place—in the company of Christian leadership in the United States. People who, like him, knew the loneliness and pressures of leading a denomination—people who *loved the Lord.*

So, when someone reached out with condolences, Troy just opened up. He told them about Greg's death, about how hard it was to meet his spouse's parents for the first time at his funeral. He cried. He spoke very simply and sweetly about his love for Greg and about how he met Greg. All the time I watched their faces. How much they did not want to be hearing this! How unaccustomed they were to this level of intimate, open, vulnerable sharing of love and grief. He pressed every homophobic, sexphobic, intimacy-phobic button they had. They looked stunned and helpless, shifting in their seats. They impatiently cleared their throats. I, too, felt helpless. I was certain that if one of them said anything to hurt him, I'd simply have to turn some tables over right there in the restaurant. Mercifully, Troy stopped. We took a breath, and Bishop Armstrong switched the subject and got down to it.

What I did not know was that not everyone at that table knew what he was about to say. The bishop leaned toward us, looked right at me, and said (I'm paraphrasing, but not too much), "I know you love Jesus Christ and the church of Jesus Christ. If you really do, you will spare us the agony of having to take a divisive vote in the fall that will only cause you pain. Please prayerfully consider withdrawing your application for membership."

I don't remember if I even looked at Troy, although I swear I could feel his blood run cold. But Armstrong had addressed me. In a flash, I pictured the dear faces of my MCC colleagues and friends as I would try to explain to them how withdrawing our application was the right thing to do, what Jesus *really* wanted. Then, thankfully, my crap detector kicked in.

Somehow I managed not to throw up the expensive salmon dinner; instead, I was able to reply. Basically, I said, "No way." Then I said something like "And don't think that by withdrawing our application it will spare us pain. Gay and lesbian people experience pain at the hands of the church of Jesus Christ every day. We are prepared to endure the pain of rejection as our cross to bear at this time in history. One of the reasons MCC is coming to the NCC is to witness visibly to the spiritual awakening in the gay and lesbian community and also to make visible the lethal homophobia of the church. We're sorry, but we think Jesus is with us in this process, and, if you do the right thing, God will be with the NCC."

That ended the discussion. Afterward, Troy let me know that he would leave the ecu-politics to me; he preferred the cutthroat secular politicians any day. But to the point of the story: sometime during that evening, I managed to spend a little time with Claire Randall. I told her about MCC's worldwide ministry, including our predominantly heterosexual churches in Nigeria among the "untouchable" people. Suddenly, she became interested. I enjoyed her questions, her interest in MCC, her insights, and what felt like her genuine respect and support of a kind. And then I asked the question. I had never personally asked this question of anyone. I chose this strange moment to ask my question of this older, close-to-retirement feminist veteran of countless ecumenical skirmishes and adventures. I remember that very private moment when I simply asked her, "Why do you think there is so much fear and resistance toward MCC?" (Really: *Why do they hate us so?*) She sighed, looked nowhere in particular, and said, "Well, I guess when you talk about sex and the Bible in the same breath, they just go nuts." Not an explanation but an excellent description: "They just go nuts."

Her statement reminded me of an incident that happened early in my ministry. When I was co-pastor at MCC Boston in 1973, I was consecrating communion on a warm summer evening. Suddenly, from the second pew, a man none of us had seen before got up, ran to the front of the sanctuary, knocked over the communion elements, punched me in the face, and ran out of the church before anyone could stop him.

They just go nuts.

Ten years later, in May 1982, I attended my first NCC governing board meeting. Adam DeBaugh, a lay leader in MCC, and I arrived in Nashville, each of us with some prior ecumenical experience but not with the NCC Governing Board. Almost 300 people met, including the press and visitors, at a large United Methodist church in Nashville. We walked in just as the opening service began. All eyes discreetly turned in our direction in a silent, dread-filled chorus of "They're here!" No one officially greeted us, and we hadn't a clue about what to do or whom to talk to.

Later that day a kindly United Methodist asked me in hushed tones, "Well, what is your strategy?" I remember feeling totally naked ("Strategy! Oh, no! I forgot to wear my strategy!"), like one of those nightmares where you show up to teach or preach without your sermon notes ... or clothing ... or something essential. We had a kind of *ecumenical innocence*. We had applied for membership and assumed we'd just go through their process. Why did we need a *strategy?* So, strategically naked, after the opening worship service, we positioned ourselves quite awkwardly, as if we were ushers or greeters, and shook hands and handed out pamphlets (like church bulletins) to Governing Board members who were leaving for a cigarette or bathroom break. Right away we were accused of being pushy. Ecumenical etiquette crashing. Some strategy! Who knew?

But—back to that opening worship service—suddenly, sitting in the last aisle in that huge church, I realized some things. The NCC and I were (and are) the same age. I thought of all it had taken to bring us together at this moment in history. Suddenly, I sensed *them* in the room: gay men and lesbians through the ages—in the churches, burned by the churches, persecuted by the churches, serving the churches, loving, and hurting. They were there. They knew I was there. I had this overwhelming sense of a mystical communion of gay and lesbian saints, some of whom had served this council in its better days. I wept for them and for us, for their longing, pain, and shame. I shed tears for their need even now for vindication and for a voice. And I felt so small, and young, and inadequate, but also so loved and watched over by them. From that moment until this, they have never left me. And many thousands have been added to their numbers.

Then everyone stood together and sang a song I had loved for a long time, the text written by an angry, questioning son of the church:

> Once to every [soul] and nation, Comes the moment to decide,
> In the strife of truth with falsehood, For the good or evil side.
> Then it is the brave [one] chooses, While the coward stands aside,

'Til the multitude make virtue, Of the faith they had denied.
By the light of burning martyrs,[5] Christ, Thy bleeding feet we track,
Toiling up new Calvaries ever, With the cross that turns not back;
New occasions teach new duties, Time makes ancient good uncouth;
They must upward still, and onward, who would
Keep abreast of truth.

—*James Russell Lowell*

The NCC members were singing our song! But did they know it yet? And, oh, *they* were also singing right along with us. The presence of my heavenly tribe sustained me that day, as it has every time an unjust structure must be challenged.

There was a place for this effort. Many heard of the Metropolitan Community Churches for the first time. Today, whole denominations that are members of the NCC have dropped their prohibitions against LGBT people. Although there is ongoing need for many of the denominations to stop oppressing LGBT people, it is their own members who are challenging them to live up to their own core values of love, justice, and respect for all God's diverse creation.

The job of MCC, its leaders, and members is to thrive as a fully inclusive, wonderfully diverse, global, and growing faith movement. We learn from our interactions with the ecumenical organizations like the NCC because our members come from so many of the traditions that belong to these Councils. Our understanding of the Bible comes from the faith traditions of our upbringing or through their influence in the broader culture. We cannot avoid grappling with well-intentioned but limited— and sometimes deadly—interpretations of scripture.

During the NCC adventure, we held three "consultations." One of these was on "Biblical Issues and Homosexuality." One of the presenters was Dr. Robin Scroggs, a New Testament Pauline scholar. He is a heterosexual scholar who has been willing to take another look at the traditional passages in Paul that have been used to condemn homosexuality and homosexuals. One of Dr. Scroggs's theses is that the New Testament simply doesn't address the situation of contemporary gay and lesbian people because, in his opinion, male homosexual relationships were in New Testament times all pederastic. In the midst of that meeting, it suddenly occurred to me that he might be suggesting that there were no ancient gay men and lesbians who had mutually consenting adult relationships. When I asked him if that was what he meant, he paused, then said, "Yes."

"How do you know that?" I asked.

His argument was one of silence. I felt this horror and rage in me that could not shut up. How could he just say that there were no people like me, like us, of our tribe, in those times? How dare he say that! How damaging it was to argue from silence.

But more than that, I had to ask myself, "How do I know we *were* there?" Judy Grahn has certainly documented us (and not as pederasts, either) in ancient history, folklore, mythology, and literature. But how did I know that day? I realized that I knew it in my guts. In my heart, in my body, and blood, and spirit, and wherever else it is that we just know things. The heavenly tribe was there, some of whom preceded New Testament times. They knew. And they now had a way of getting my attention. Dr. Scroggs's well-meaning remark, his theories, *seemed* harmless enough on the surface. But to me they were something akin to genocide. I felt all this terrible grief at the suggestion that *they* (we) had not been there all along. Closeted, for sure—quiet, oppressed, silent—but *there*.

The Bible is infused with identity, and identity always informs our interpretation—our hermeneutic—of scripture. Ancient Israel had a complex process of identity formation. Who are the Jews in the Bible? Are they a race or a tribe, a religion or a nation, a culture or a set of traditions? They are a people with a vague prehistory. They were shaped by the historical crucibles of the Exodus and Exile; by courageous leaders, common oppression, and covenant values; by storytellers and events. They were forged from an amalgam of tribes, rituals, and stories.

It was they who wrote down their journeys and stories so that future generations would remember. They were a tribe torn between, on one hand, welcoming strangers, caring for orphans and widows, and, on the other hand, defending their boundaries and identities and being aggressive warriors for Yahweh—God Almighty.

They were like all the tribes in the ancient lands. They were defined by the god of their ancestors and would live and die by their faith.

There is a certain critical tension about this *tribal identity thing*. I remember reading death-of-God theologian Richard Rubenstein's book *After Auschwitz* when I was in college. I recall his searching questions about the implications of the Jewish concept of chosenness, its permutations in Christian thought, and the terribly twisted notions of chosenness that characterized the Nazi doctrine of Aryan supremacy. He asked if the concept of chosenness, no matter how humble or benign, might lead inevitably to doctrines of exclusiveness and superiority.

To many, of course, Rubenstein's critique sounded all too much like *blaming the victim*. However, his critique of what I call "tribal ontology" is perhaps more relevant than ever in these days of global ethnic conflicts and growing fundamentalism.

The dilemma of tribal theology and tribal biblical hermeneutics is discussed at length in the book *Out of Every Tribe and Nation* by Justo Gonzales. On the one hand, notes Gonzales, "there is always the likelihood that any theology that claims to be *universal* is no more than theology from the particular perspective of those who are in power."[6] In other words, the dominant tribes set the agenda, and get to "universalize" *their* tribal theology. On the other hand, there is the danger of what he calls the "romanticization of culture," in which groups may "idealize [their] culture as if it were perfect and did not stand in need of correction from the gospel."[7] No culture is free from human problems and divisions. There has to be a delicate balance between the search for universal truth and the context of tribal particularity.

So, do gay and lesbian people identify more with our tribe(s) or more with our humanness? In recent years, we have been fighting for our rights and gaining many of them. Straight allies who support us are pushed forward to help fence sitters see the light. Our families are increasingly part of the larger culture. MCC congregations are comprised of LGBTQ people and straight families and individuals who want to be part of the church universal—not the church prejudicial. Our identities are more complex than ever.

The academic world has critiqued "identity politics" as dated and a product of a past that did not really understand diversity and multilayered identities. This dismissal of our past movement work does a disservice to the thousands of people who marched with me in 1972. I walked among those who were the backbone of the movement—and joined in. The terminology may have changed, but we were in the thick of understanding our multifaceted and multiplying identities. Movement leaders of the 1960s and 1970s were no less effective at challenging the layers of racial, gender, and class realities of their day than progressives are today. Can they be critiqued? Certainly. Were they imperfect? Absolutely! Were they committed to justice and working to eliminate oppression. No doubt! The same as folks are today.

To be fair, each generation must come to its own insights. It is the same with the Bible. Generations in the Bible added new insights and perspectives and sometimes critiqued "old" ways of doing things or just adapted to their new context—whether it was moving from nomadic ways to agrarian ways or from freedom to exile. New books were written, reforms were implemented, and the tribe took on new life.

But, like the Israelites, we are a tribe rooted in the experience of exile. We were formed out of being exiled from our tribes of birth—our families, our churches, our communities—for being queer. For many, rejection is turning to acceptance, but most of us still make decisions day-to-day about who we can trust and how we can live our lives safely with our families. It is still too easy to internalize the hatred. Teen suicide and homelessness have not gone away.

Many years ago, Rev. Troy Perry wrote, in an open letter to the church (from *The Lord Is My Shepherd and He* [sic] *Knows I'm Gay*), "I am not a creature from the other darkness, I am a man of flesh and blood."[8] In many places in the world, it is our humanness as gay, lesbian, and transgender people that is still the issue. In the United States, even while marriage equality is in place for more than 30 percent of the total population, 30 states have declared our marriages unconstitutional. Evangelists routinely blame us for natural and unnatural disasters. We have come so far and still have so much work to do—and how the Bible is interpreted is foundational to our future.

The Queers in the Queer Hermeneutic

Who are gay men, lesbians, bisexual, and transgender people? To bring a queer hermeneutic, we need to have some sense about who the queers are in the queer hermeneutic. Sometimes, in my deepest self, I feel like we are some ancient tribal remnant that has survived and that now appears to be dispersed among every other earthly tribe—a transtribal tribe!

But others see our lives as simply a matter of despised behavior(s). Then there's all the hypothalamus hype: genetics, brain components. The truth is, we talk about being queer in many ways. Some of us do believe that we chose our orientation and gender identity. Most, in my experience, speak of it more in terms of a discovery—a gift given before we were aware of receiving it.

For me, being a lesbian was not a choice. The only choice was how I would or would not accept who I was. And it was not *only* a discovery. For me—and this is admittedly romantic —it has also felt like my *destiny*. Martin Buber said, "We must believe in Destiny, and that it stands in need of us."[9]

In June of 1972, I marched down Fifth Avenue with my lesbian friend Jean in one of New York's earliest Gay Pride parades. I'd only been out of the closet for three months. And there I was walking down Fifth Avenue next to Jill Johnston, author of *Lesbian Nation,* and the original "queer nation," and author Isabel Miller. I don't think I ever closed my mouth for four hours.

The most queers I'd ever seen in one place together before that had been maybe five or six. That day, we were at least 50,000 people: drag queens, leather queens, lesbian separatists—a raucous, irreverent, heart-pounding throng. We marched breathing fire and freedom.

As we moved up Fifth Avenue, I fell in love with this movement. Whatever part of me that still had doubts, still wondered if I was not just in love with this *one* particular woman—just a phase, a fluke—evaporated in the steamy June New York Sunday afternoon heat. Everyone smiled at everyone; we delighted in one another, no strangers among us. It felt like my tribal initiation. I knew we were made in the image of God!

Years later, I visited All God's Children MCC Minneapolis and witnessed a new phenomenon: a gay men's softball team. Now, lesbian softball is legendary and an undisputed part of lesbian culture in the United States. But a gay male team? MCC Minneapolis had three teams: two lesbian, and one composed of young gay men with shaved, punk haircuts, earrings, and muscled bodies. They had a very cute team name—The Altared Boys—and great T-shirts that said:

MADE IN THE IMAGE OF GOD—
not necessarily
YOUR IMAGE OF GOD!

I believe that gay and lesbian people contribute to a more complete picture of God. If the Bible starts with establishing that human beings are made in the image of God, then that includes gay men and lesbians. What about us rounds out the image, do you suppose? The God who invented truth is always *coming out* (another synonym for revelation?).

I've always felt that God has a sense of humor. Much of the humor in the Bible has long since been lost in the translation, quite literally. But "he [sic] who sits in the heavens laughs" (Psalms 2:4). Sometimes I think God plays with me, and we have had some private jokes. For a long time, I was afraid to say that out loud. It seemed either too grandiose or too unsophisticated to think that God would affectionately joke with me. But the humor is undeniable.

Just looking at the cast of characters in the Bible—the philandering bisexual David, the bold prophets, the often dense disciples of Jesus, the befuddled religious leaders who were always trying to trick Jesus. Whether or not the characters are funny, they all have elements of irony, surprise, and poignancy.

In my life, sometimes funny is just the incredible, illogical synchronicity of things. I was driving home from Fort Wayne to Detroit at a moment in one of the worst years of my life when some nightmarish events and problems in the church had me exhausted, demoralized. In the words of Al-Anon literature, I was "unwanted, unloved, and alone"—and feeling sorry for myself. I turned on the radio and heard Billy Joel's "Just the Way You Are." Later, I would learn that Billy was from my home town of Hicksville, New York. Billy's Long Island accent was poignantly familiar and tugged at me on that lonely road—along with the words and the saxophone. I changed the station, and the song came on again. That startled me. A new popular tune, I guess! I listened to the words again, full of sweet assurances. I began to have this eerie feeling of not being alone in the car. I could feel the tightness in my chest relax and the sadness and depression lift for a moment. In a little while I turned the dial again—and there it was again. This time it scared me. Okay, I thought, it's you. You love me. The tears came, I started laughing, "Okay, okay, God, you love me. You want to talk to me."

But it didn't stop there. It seemed that it was playing every time I walked into a room where a radio was playing. Other people even noticed it. This went on for months and months. Paula and I were walking through Boston Commons the following summer (we had met just three weeks after my drive from Fort Wayne that night), and a guy was playing that song on a xylophone! Even today, that sweet song appears and interrupts me, especially if I'm feeling a little unwanted, a little unloved, or alone. I don't pretend to understand it; I don't, but I'm trying to accept it. The words and tune just sort of befriended me, as a precious gift from a God who thinks I'm too sophisticated for my own good a lot of the time.

God's humor and tender love reminds those of us who feel on the outside that we are needed. We hold up the mirror of reflection to the church especially. We are, after all, the "in-between" folks. We've been both very much on the inside of the church (as its organists, choir directors, pastors, board members, deacons, bishops) and on the outside, trying to learn how to "embrace the exile," in John Fortunato's famous phrase.

At a World Council of Churches Assembly, Rev. Steve Pieters was wearing a lavender clergy shirt and waiting in the lobby for a meeting to begin. An older Australian delegate approached him and said, "In our church, when someone wears that color clergy shirt it means they are a bishop!"

To this comment, Steve replied, "In our church, it means we are gay!" (That's not entirely accurate, but Steve was being playful.)

The woman did *not* skip a beat and rejoined, "I guess that's what it means in our church, too!"

Being "in-between" is a place of both wisdom and humor. When we see the contradictions, we learn to live in the midst of them. They can make us laugh, and they can make us cry. Over the years, people have sometimes commented on my irreverence. Frankly, I hold back a lot—not because I think God will be offended, but because I don't want to be more misunderstood than I already am. But I see irreverence mostly as *play.* When you really trust someone, you can kid that person. You know how far to go. I feel like I have that kind of relationship with God.

My grandfather, part Indian and part reluctant Baptist, had that kind of relationship with God. In one of the few private conversations we ever had, he told me on the way home from church one day that I "should not take this church stuff too seriously." He went on to say that it seemed to him that anyone (namely, Jesus) who would change water into wine must have enjoyed himself now and then. Don't let them take all the joy out of life. "Them," I figured, meant preachers and other religious folks. My grandfather already knew that I was attracted to this "church stuff," and he worried about me because of it! I think he is still a source of my irreverence and my desire for a lighter touch at times.

Church ought to be a place where people are loved, comforted, and uplifted, but also a place where we are shocked, shaken, and turned around—and a place where we can laugh. I'm not talking about giggling or chuckling; I mean deep, roll-in-the-aisles laughing. Not every Sunday perhaps, but frequently. In the Middle Ages, it was the custom to begin every Easter Sunday morning sermon with a joke. It was the day above all days when we were to laugh in church, to laugh at the devil who had been utterly defeated and outsmarted.

In most MCC churches, there will be laughter—in some, a great deal of laughter. Maybe this started because many of us were nervous about being in church and being ourselves all at the same time. Some MCC services can have just a hint of the barroom rowdiness that is a leftover from the time when noisy, crowded bars were the only places we were more or less permitted to meet. For some people, MCC is the only place where they are out of the closet or where they can hold their partner's hand in public or wear leather and chains. We used to have endless arguments about that. What is proper church etiquette in a gay and lesbian church that is open to everyone? Why do people sometimes behave like they are in a bar when they are in a church? Well, it's a cultural thing, I think. And it helps make MCC a little less *threatening* to people who are frightened of or allergic to too much church.

MCC also serves a healthy dose of charismatic theology, worship, and piety, without the usual narrowness and fundamentalism. This is because MCC's roots are thoroughly working class, and many of our members are from that style of worship.

For many years, MCC Long Beach, California, hosted a charismatic conference. I tried never to miss it. There is nothing quite like seeing several hundred gay, lesbian, and bisexual charismatics (or those dabbling in it for the weekend) worshipping, weeping, singing, holding, sweating, and hugging each other, unashamed of their love for God and each other.

One year after a major controversy at MCC Los Angeles over names for God, I attended the Saturday evening service at the charismatic conference. I was having a difficult time. I was recovering from gall bladder surgery and a church fight. I had also just lost 30 pounds in a fast. There were many in my family and MCC who did not understand why I had fasted. I had had a lot of support, but I had also been through a lot of hell that year.

The guest speaker was a powerful, heterosexual woman, Erla Duncan, known in charismatic circles for her gifts of knowledge, prophecy, and healing. She is a short woman with a big voice and a rather imposing presence. Erla had taken a lot of heat in her ministry for not condemning gay and lesbian people and for being willing to teach and preach in our churches. It was amazing to watch her. She would call on you (in front of 300 people!) and just start talking about you to you or prophesying about you. Neither you nor she had any idea of what was going to happen. She'd talk, and people would begin to cry, or shout, or pray. That night she pointed to me. I stood, feeling like a very nervous six-year-old girl. She prophesied that I would be given opportunities to speak in arenas of national importance, and lots of other things. But then she paused and said, in a booming voice, "But, oh, the devil hates you! In fact, they have weekly meetings about you!" When she said that to me, my face reddened, but the crowd roared. And then I began to laugh. And I couldn't stop laughing. In fact, I laughed all the way home that night. I laughed on the way to church the next day. I laughed about it for weeks, off and on. What a great, sweeping, overwhelming relief!

I did not grow up with theological language that ever talked much about the *devil*, and when I first encountered it in people at MCC, it made me nervous. I still haven't sorted out all those issues. But I do know that God has enemies, whatever you choose to call them or it. And if I am God's friend, those forces and folks will also see me as their enemy. I do believe that if you "resist the devil, he [sic] will flee from you" (James 4:7); but, first, he or she will try to make life miserable for you. Once I was willing to face that *some* of the hell I had been going through was because I had resisted evil, because I had tried to move some terribly stubborn mountains, I was so relieved. Like all folks (including ancient shamans) who do such things, I had to pay a price for it. But, ultimately, I was and am safe. Erla Duncan's word to me that night was God's word to me, delivered in the kind of humorous, irreverent way I could recognize. Weekly meetings! Hah!

At a lecture once, one of the participants said to me, "You are so irreverent, you make me want to read the Bible."

Most gay and lesbian people do not want to read the Bible. And I don't blame them! They assume, like most people, that the Bible is not exactly our friend or best supporter! They believe that it is, at best, irrelevant to our lives or, at worst, our enemy, condemning us to hell.

Robert Goss, in *Jesus Acted Up*,[10] first used the title of Phyllis Trible's book, *Texts of Terror*,[11] to identify the six Bible passages quoted by fundamentalists and uninformed Christians to condemn homosexuality.[12] These have become our "texts of terror." Their existence, combined with millennia of misinterpretation, has formed a powerful wedge, keeping lesbians and gay men away from being able to celebrate and experience the story and poetry of the Bible.

If we dust off an old Bible or actually go out and buy a new one to read, it should come with a warning label. There are rich veins of tradition and story to be mined in the Bible—and there are also *minefields*. Books about the Bible and other "helpful" reading materials are not necessarily accessible, or they are written from theological perspectives that are sexist or otherwise oppressive; or they are so incredibly technical that you have to have a Ph.D. in theology to read them.

This frustrates me. Even people who are not sure they believe in God could benefit from knowing something about the Bible. The Bible is still used politically. Traditional interpretations of the Bible still inform popular notions about a God who condemns. These ideas influence politics, relationships, and attitudes in cultures here and around the world.

For gay and lesbian people, this is especially crucial. I want not only to disarm the Bible bashers but to find a way to turn *their swords* (Bible stories and passages) *into plowshares*. I even thought of calling this section of the book "Rescuing the Bible from Heterosexual Bigots," following a little bit in John Shelby Spong's footsteps.[13]

I hear story after story of gay and lesbian adults walking into church supply and bookstores for the first time, finding it difficult to believe that they are actually there. They are prepared with our advice on what translation to buy. Touching and holding a book that they have always believed was a source of pain and condemnation, they dare to open the book, hoping and hungry. Joy emerges as they begin to appreciate its complexity and as they mine the treasures and negotiate the minefields.

This is also true with the communion. One of the most powerful experiences I have as a pastor is the privilege of training MCC student clergy and deacons in how to consecrate communion. (Deacons are an order of lay ministry in MCC; they may perform many of the rites and sacraments of the church, as well as preach, teach, and provide lay pastoral care for members.) It is positively redemptive to watch gay men and lesbians take the elements of communion representing the Body and Blood of Christ *into their own hands,* quite literally. Their experience of inclusion and empowerment is intoxicating and healing. As they touch the bread and juice, say the ancient words, and preside over this liturgy for the sake of their own people, they become transformed. They are never the same.

Whether it is the Bible or communion, we bring our interpretations and the interpretation of our family and community with us.

I really appreciate Virginia Mollenkott's chapter on "Building Bridges between Interpretative Communities" from her book *Sensuous Spirituality.*[14] Among the important things that she says helps develop gay and lesbian biblical interpretative method:

> Every human being belongs to an interpretative community. Inevitably, we must communicate from within specific situations. And to be in a specific situation is to be possessed by a "structure of assumptions, of practices understood to be relevant in relation to purposes and goals that are already in place."

Mollenkott goes on to cite Stanley Fish's study called "Is There a Text in This Class? The Authority of Interpretative Communities":

> Stanley Fish explains that "the self does not exist apart from the communal or conventional categories of thought that enable its operations (of thinking, seeing, reading)." Because all "conceptions that fill consciousness . . . are culturally derived," there is no such thing as a wholly free consciousness. Nobody's interpretive acts are exclusively her own; our interpretations fall to us by virtue of our position "in some socially organized environment."[15]

Mollenkott identifies herself with the "liberation theology" interpretative community and builds bridges with evangelicals, feminists, and others. She states:

> In each community [of biblical interpretation], there is an agreement (often unwritten and unspoken) about what

constitutes evidence and what is irrelevant or beside the point....
It is futile for us to fling accusations at each other about creating
"a canon within the canon" (that is, emphasizing some Scriptures and jumping over others), because every interpretative
community tends to do the same.

When gay and lesbian people first started publicly challenging the traditional reading of the Bible, we were (and still are) vilified for reading
and interpreting the Bible for ourselves. As an example, I would like to
quote from a letter we received at MCC headquarters in 1993, not from
a fundamentalist but from a member of the Central Committee of the
World Council of Churches:

> I was aghast and appalled at the thinly veiled attempt to twist
> the Bible and Christian message in what seems to me to be a
> dishonest, heretical, and even blasphemous manner. I wonder
> why those of you who believe in homosexuality are straining to
> give it some semblance of respectability by deliberately misin-
> terpreting the Christian message. I do not have the time to take
> you up one by one on the heresies and blasphemies contained
> in the documents you sent.... I, as well as all those who read
> their Bibles without jaundiced eyes, am firmly convinced that
> HOMOSEXUALITY is both a SIN and an ABNORMALITY.
> [Emphasis in the original]

So, are we stuck in simply reading the Bible in the context of our interpretative communities? Is there no *objective way* to read the Bible? I think
there is not a *neutral* place from which to read and interpret the Bible.
However, as Mollenkott states, there is the hope of building bridges across
interpretative communities.

Some of our communities are very new at this work of biblical interpretation. We need to be free to experiment, try on new ideas, even make
mistakes, change our minds, and say the outrageous, without being labeled "heretical" or "blasphemous."

The scare words of *heresy* and *blasphemy* are painfully familiar to women,
gay, lesbian, bisexual, and transgender people. They are the tools of white
heterosexual male domination, especially in the areas of theology and biblical interpretation. They are about control and intellectual terrorism.

One of the things I hope to accomplish, however, is to *move away from just defending ourselves* (and our right to engage in biblical texts so that they are not *just* a source of pain for our people) into a more proactive reading of the Bible. Elisabeth Schussler-Fiorenza, in her groundbreaking work *In Memory of Her,* states, "The explorations of this book begin therefore with the hope of moving away from the pervasive apologetic that characterizes most treatments of women in the Bible to a historical-critical reconstruction of women's history and women's contributions to early Christian beginnings."[16]

Moving away from apologetics to "historical-critical reconstructions" is what I hope to *begin,* more than accomplish. For gay and lesbian people, this is more than just a matter of reevaluating our role. We first have to *back up and just begin to document our existence!*

John Boswell has done this quite remarkably in his books *Christianity, Social Tolerance, and Homosexuality* and *Same-Sex Unions in Pre-Modern Europe.*[17] Boswell describes his research on same-sex unions as this amazing process of following a hunch, looking for hints of the existence of actual same-sex couple ceremonies in the Middle Ages. As he followed his hunches, the evidence appeared mysteriously, miraculously. Once he began to believe in the existence of these couples, it was as if they began to appear and to document themselves!

I feel a kinship to Boswell's work in my own work of uncovering our existence in the Bible. One has to break through the barrier of homophobic perception first and *really believe we have always been here.* When we do that, our faith is rewarded. It was pure delight to read the Vatican's (and Eastern Orthodox) mutterings and mumblings and whines about how Boswell's research couldn't possibly prove what it clearly proves! Gays and lesbians have existed, even with the church's blessing, in other times! What has not been done enough, however, is even to document the presence and role of queer people in the Bible, and in a positive sense. Mostly, we've been content with trying to prove that the Bible does not unilaterally condemn us.

There is a certain tension about simply facing the patriarchal context and homophobic possibilities of the Holy Bible. For if it was written in a patriarchal, homophobic context, then it is not only the interpretation of the Bible but also the content itself that contributes to oppressive ideas about us. Is our purpose to refute what the Bible actually says about gays and lesbians? Or to uncover and expose *assumptions* about what is really said? To *redeem* the Bible or to *redeem our community*? Or can both be done? And can one be done without the other?

Fiorenza takes what may be or may appear to be a very radical position in relationship to the Bible when she says:

> A feminist theological hermeneutics [interpretative method] having as its canon the liberation of women from oppressive patriarchal texts, structures, institutions, and values maintains that—if the Bible is not to continue as a tool for the patriarchal oppression of women—only those traditions and texts that critically break through patriarchal culture and "plausibility structures" bear the theological authority of revelation. The "advocacy stance" of liberation theologies cannot accord revelatory authority to any oppressive and destructive biblical text or tradition. Nor did they have any such claim at any point in history; such critical measure must be applied to all biblical texts, their historical contexts, and theological interpretations and not just to the texts on women.[18]

In plainer English: a feminist interpretation of scripture will be upfront concerning being selective about which texts will be authoritative *for* women *about* women. Scripture passages that oppress women are not now, nor have they ever been, holy or authoritative for women. Because women did not have the resources or power to write or study the Bible, or to vote on the canon of scripture, we have to do that now, after the fact.

This particular political stance in biblical interpretation presses the alarm buttons of those who feel it is blasphemy to distinguish among biblical texts, or to be willing to ignore some. It might also seem to validate the claims of those who accuse feminists, liberation theologians, and gays and lesbians of "picking and choosing" only the parts of the Bible that support our point of view. Of course what Mollenkott and Fiorenza and others say is that we've *all* been doing that *all* along! Only now, at last, it's our turn.

Although parts of the Bible have *never* been and *never will be* revelatory for me (they are obviously misogynist, or violent, or just obscure, or not very interesting), they may serve as very important reminders, as documentation of the history of oppression and the source of our struggles. They, too, are a part of our tribal memory.

For this reason—that *we may never forget*—it is still important for gay and lesbian people to understand how the Bible has been misused to oppress us. It is part of the de-shaming and healing of our community.

This healing must include the love many of us have had for the Bible. It seems to me that I have always loved the Bible. But I was not always sure that it would love me back.

I remember reading the first Bible I got in Methodist Sunday school. I was determined to read it cover to cover. The print was small. I had no commentary, and weekly Sunday school lessons barely skimmed the surface of biblical stories. I read and read through long, boring, disappointing passages. Often I would come across things that were odd, frightening, or unintelligible. There were lots of endless descriptive details and hard-to-pronounce names and lists. But every now and then I stumbled on a book, chapter, or verse of pure gold, worth all my perseverance. As a lonely 12-year-old girl, I had lots of time for this endeavor.

I loved Cranston Clayton's sermons at Hicksville Methodist Church. In his folksy Tennessee drawl, he preached a fervent, anti-fundamentalist, biblical, social Gospel. He preached the Bible story, week after week, from a lectionary of his own creating. Anticipating the biblical illiteracy of a new generation, he retold the Bible for us. He even gave us a *living Bible map:* the parking lot was the Mediterranean Sea, the sanctuary was Israel, the gymnasium was Greece and Europe, and the offices were Egypt! His Bible characters were alive with poignancy and passion. I particularly appreciated that he didn't shy away from the juicier parts.

Clayton didn't care for children very much. He expected that, if you were a child sitting through his sermons (which I sometimes did twice on Sundays), you had better listen like an adult. Oh, the way he *told* the stories of David and Bathsheba, Peter and Paul and Silas, Jesus and Mary Magdalene, made me *want* to preach.

I wanted to make people feel the way he made me feel—like I was right there in those stories, in the thick of the battles, the miracles, smelling the smoke from the burning bush, touching Jesus, feeling Deborah's strength and conviction. I loved the tears, laughter, tales of mercy and cruelty, the scandal, the surprises. He acted, agonized, mused, imagined, and painted verbal murals. Also, he seemed to have access to some mysterious repository of *inside information,* important details *missing* from the text itself. I never mistrusted his special source and the way he filled in the gaps.

So at age 14 I asked my dad to take me to talk to Clayton about becoming a preacher. Clayton just looked at me—the way people squint at people who are somehow barely visible to them. Because I knew he didn't like or take notice of kids, and because I was female, I already knew in my heart that talking to him was a long shot. He spoke to my father mostly. "Aw," he said, "she'll be just like my daughter: go to seminary, marry some preacher, and it will all be wasted on her." My dad, who had a hard enough time just getting to the pastor's office in the first place (it made him nervous), just sat silently. When I pressed Clayton (making him talk to *me*), he finally grunted and gave me the name and address of a woman Methodist minister he knew about in Kansas. End of discussion.

I wrote to her the next day. She eventually wrote back. It turned out that she had been married to a minister. When he died, she finally got to go to seminary and got ordained. (She was now in her sixties.) Somehow, I didn't think I could wait that long—or that I should have to. It did occur to me, in a fleeting way, that I could just marry a very old, sick man and kind of get that part out of the way real early. But that seemed grotesque to me. I had also wanted to ask Clayton why he thought God would put ideas about preaching into girls' heads if it was all just going to be a waste. And I had this other feeling that I couldn't explain and already knew not to verbalize: that being married to a man was going to be the least of my problems.

Poor Clayton, he knew the Bible very well. He just didn't know anything about young lesbians who loved the Bible. Mind you, Clayton was not above making homophobic comments. He didn't watch a lot of TV. (How could he? He had to be reading the Bible all the time and figuring out which parts we ought to hear about!) But I remember that in one sermon he talked about two brand-new TV hits. They were "doctor" shows in the early Sixties: about *Ben Casey* and *Dr. Kildare*. Ben Casey was a swarthy, hyper-masculine sex symbol. Dr. Kildare was blond and delicate.

Clayton decided to talk about how he didn't care for Dr. Kildare, who was too namby-pamby (read *queer*). He thought Jesus was probably more *rugged* (read *macho*), like hairy old Ben Casey. I remember my strong reaction to Clayton that morning. I took it very personally and wasn't sure why—partly because I liked Richard Chamberlain, who played Kildare and is an openly gay man today. I already knew that I liked boys or men better when they were pretty or a little more like girls. Hairy men kinda scared me. My dad was muscular and strong but had very little body hair (in fact, we always joked about his seven measly chest hairs). He always said it was because his father was part Indian. My dad was soft-spoken and managed, even with scarred hands from being a mechanic, to be gentle in his touch and manner. When I got to preach, I thought, I would make Jesus be more like Dr. Kildare. Maybe not so blond, but kind of soft and pretty like Richard Chamberlain—like my dad, or maybe like one of the women teachers I had a crush on.

Aside from the Ben Casey versus Jim Kildare fiasco, Clayton seemed right about a lot of things to me. For instance, he said that Dr. Martin Luther King Jr. was a lot like Jesus (and, by the way, not at all like Ben Casey or Jim Kildare!) and that we ought to be a lot nicer to Catholics (in those early Vatican II years).

Somehow, the Bible was in favor of all of this, and if I just kept at it long enough, I would find all that good stuff eventually.

It has taken me decades to find the *really good stuff*, which is part of the purpose of this book. The world needs to hear the stories. For this, I thank Clayton.

In about 1978, Dr. Norman Pittenger came to preach at MCC Detroit. He made an astonishing comment: "Actually, the Bible is a greatly overrated book." This still makes me wince and laugh. I picture all those people, over all those millennia, spending their lives poring over, studying, and translating a *greatly overrated book*. Working hard to improve its *ratings!* Is that what we do? What I'm doing? Feminist icon and theologian, Mary Daly, once told me she thought that the feminist passages in the Bible would make an interesting *pamphlet*.

So, is the Bible an angel I'm wrestling until it blesses me and all gay and lesbian people? Am I just locked in a lifelong "lovers' quarrel" with this book?

I preached my first sermon in seventh grade, in Mrs. Gitlitz's English class. We each had to give a ten-minute speech. Mine was entitled "The Bible and the Science Book: Do They Conflict?" I loved science, especially biology, evolution, and astronomy. It seemed so clear to me that both atheistic views of science and anti-intellectual, anti-scientific, fundamentalist views of the Bible were unsatisfactory. I had this passionate desire to communicate this to my peers—most of whom, frankly, couldn't have cared less. Maybe I was passionate because I was one of the only Protestants in my school and neighborhood, and I already knew that others associated the Bible and *all* Protestants with fundamentalism.

My speech did cause a stir among faculty and administration at the school. In that time of challenges about school prayer and the need to create religious tolerance and address the biased perception of Protestant hegemony, it became impossible even to mention religion in the classroom. In my sermon-speech, I had broken the rule. How my heart pounded. How I longed to talk about these issues with someone—anyone. I petitioned the school to have an after-school "club" that could discuss religion. They gave me permission. Steffi, my friend from English class, came—not because she wanted to talk about religion (she was an agnostic) but because she wanted to support me. She thought I was so brave! Four of us met a few times in the library, so it never amounted to much. But I thought a lot about how much pain it must cause God to be misunderstood and misrepresented. And God liked the truth. So why were *people* afraid of the truth?

It never mattered to me whether or not the Bible was accurate as to facts. For some reason, I never equated fact and truth. It never worried me whether the Bible was literally true. Miraculously, I trusted my own heart. My heart leapt equally at the wonders of the cell, the solar system, and the poetry and power of a biblical story. I love the idea of reading what ancient humans of faith felt when they saw the same creation.

Sometime during this time I saw the movie *Inherit the Wind*. I thought that God must have loved the brilliant, free-thinking, doubting, questioning lovers of justice and seekers of truth like Clarence Darrow. God enjoyed them more than the mean-spirited, self-righteous ones who hated under cover of biblical infallibility.

I remember fantasizing about a special place of reconciliation in heaven for God and all the atheists and agnostics who, out of love for God's creation and people, rejected perverse human notions of God—especially those supposedly supported by the Bible. There was also a part of me that sometimes fantasized about a special place in hell for religious folks who used the Bible abusively to hurt, alienate, and create an atmosphere of violence toward others. It is hard to accept this memory of my own capacity for cruel imaginings—especially because I believed there really could not be a *hell*. (Although, I still wonder, what *did* God do with Adolf Hitler?) It was difficult to reconcile my universalism with the endless human capacity for destruction and cruelty. Reluctantly, I made myself imagine their redemption and their healing. Mostly I wanted to access for myself and others the mysterious, poignant, tender, sweet, funny, and helpful stuff in the Bible, to loosen and lighten it up.

I was hoping for that type of engagement when, some years ago, I spoke at the college I had graduated from—Allegheny College in Meadville, Pennsylvania. I did so as an open lesbian alumna! At my lecture on "Outing the Bible," biblical literalists pounded me with a barrage of questions. They were outwardly polite, white, mostly middle-class students, wide-eyed with sincerity. I tried to understand their intensity and fear. For some of them, intellectual exchange and "agreeing to disagree" were tolerable. But others simply hammered at me rhetorically, as if trying to break me under the weight of their questions. As if, just listening to them read from their Bible, I would fall down on my knees in front of them and repent! Students who, I assumed (perhaps falsely), could tolerate ambiguity, fine distinction, and unresolved questions in other areas of inquiry could *not* do so with the Bible.

The atmosphere became ritualistic, cult-like, as one young woman repeated over and over again that if one could *speculate* (I had enraged her by using the word) about homosexuals in the Bible, then one could *speculate* about *anything* in the Bible! (This apparently would ruin it!) When I replied that I didn't find the word *speculate* to be a bad word and asked just what she was so afraid of, her intensity increased. It was as if these young students believed the Bible to be a fragile magic snow castle ready to melt—or a row of dominoes ready to fall with the first invading question.

For me, the Bible is an elastic, resilient friend who bounces back and even talks back when I question it. I can still see how the "biblically impaired" male student shook with rage at my really rather harmless attempts to see gays and lesbians in the Bible. The demons of homophobia screeched at me through him that night.

It would be so much easier for these students if we gays and lesbians would just continue to hate ourselves and the Bible. If, like Job's wife, these students, and all who believe the way they do, could just get us to curse God and die—no problem!

But it's not their Bible or their God to control. The Bible belongs to anyone who will love it, play with it, push it to its limits, touch it, and be touched by it—and the same is true for God. The Bible *must* be a holy text for gays and lesbians, because we are truly human, created by the God who created heaven and earth. We are called to a critical question: Will we believe what others have told us about the Bible, feel awful about it and ourselves (and possibly reject the Bible or devalue ourselves), or will we dare to learn and study and struggle with our own canon? The choice is ours.

2 • A Lesbian Hermeneutic Of Suspicion

I am borrowing from Fiorenza in daring to speak of a "lesbian hermeneutic of suspicion." LGBT people, using all the tools of feminist and liberation scholarship, must dare to push against the biblical silences and clues about homosexuality.

When a "traditional" hermeneutic of absolute truth is used, we are subjected to the practice of unquestioning condemnation and persecution of lesbian and gay people that has passed for "truth" for far too long.

Using a hermeneutic of suspicion, we approach the text with a suspicion that the accepted interpretations are flawed—and that texts that reflect our lives have been ignored and suppressed.

We must find the ways to expose the heterosexist biases of most Bible translations and commentaries, and to be willing to discover the ways in which the Bible already provides us with all the necessary materials to develop a gay and lesbian interpretative method (hermeneutic).

In that vein, if it is true that "every interpretative method works to perpetuate some ideology," then it is fair to say that until very recently most, if not all, methods used to interpret the Bible have perpetuated the ideology of heterosexism.

For most people who have read or heard of the Bible, their unqualified assumption is that the Bible condemns homosexuality and homosexuals. People have the same certainty about this that they once had about the Bible's support for the subordination of women and the biblical justification of slavery and racism.

Part of the politics of biblical interpretation is the fact that some Bible passages and concepts get studied while others do not. What gets studied, published, recorded, and taught is what institutions and authorities (usually religious ones) will permit and fund. Basically, that is, we explore what the dominant culture will support.

A hundred years ago, a daring group of feminist amateur Bible scholars wrote *The Women's Bible*. But, it took nearly a hundred years before male-dominated seminaries would finally support, permit, and fund women biblical scholars to study the Bible in a way that challenges thousands of years of misogynist assumptions and biblical interpretation. In a parallel way, 100 years earlier, black liberation theology writers began to move beyond the reinterpretation of the "curse of Ham" in the book of Genesis. But it took a long time to fund African-American biblical scholarship.

In comparison, it was only in 1955 when D. S. Bailey's *Homosexuality and the Western Christian Tradition* was published, the first book ever to challenge the negative assumptions about homosexuality in the Bible. The birth and growth of the gay and lesbian secular and spiritual movement have begun to demand revision of traditional views of homosexuality and the Bible. Now, scores of books and hundreds of articles by scholars, historians, and literary folk have joined Bailey's first heroic effort, including Jeff Miner and Tyler Connoley's excellent *The Children Are Free*.

However, even after more than 60 years of biblical critique and research, the assumption in the popular mind still reigns supreme that the Bible condemns homosexuality. Too many Christians are not aware that there is *any other point of view.*

This moves us beyond the politics of biblical interpretation to the politics of the church and its responsibility to teach what it knows.

In the 1980s, I participated in a series of well-organized "consultations" jointly sponsored by the National Council of Churches of Christ in the U.S.A. and the MCC. These consultations were commissioned by the Governing Board of the NCC in the aftermath of their decision to "postpone indefinitely" their vote on MCC's eligibility for membership in the NCC. These three consultations were to be about subjects believed to be major areas of disagreement between MCC and member communions of the NCC (and, more to the point, among and between those communions). The subjects were biblical interpretations of homosexuality, the science of human sexuality, and ecclesiology (the study of the church).

We tackled the biblical consultation first. I served as one of two MCC persons on the steering committee for the consultations. Our preparation included gathering the names of requested scripture scholars "in the guild" who had published on this subject and who would be willing to speak publicly to the NCC and MCC. The idea was to get scholars on "both sides of the issue" in order to have "balance."

After some time had passed, NCC members of the steering committee informed us that they were able to find several suitable scholars to speak on the side of supporting a revised view of homosexuality and the Bible but could find no one who would speak on the more traditional side of the issue. We in MCC responded by providing several names of scholars familiar to us who are known for their traditional views on this subject. The NCC folks countered by saying that none of those "scholars" was acceptable, as they were not represented in the "guild" of Scripture scholars or did not come from the churches of the NCC.

Finally, the steering committee proceeded by asking an Old Testament and New Testament scholar to be the presenters, Drs. Robin Scroggs and Bruce Schaefer. Both Scroggs and Schaefer presented information and conclusions that support MCC's position on homosexuality and the Bible. Dr. Schaefer said during his presentation, "No serious Bible scholar would make the statement that the Bible unilaterally condemns homosexuality." That was the first time I ever recall any scholar making that statement. I thought it was probably the most important outcome of the consultation. Frankly, I thought it should be front-page news. But of course it never made it to the front page or even to the back page.

Our committee was permitted to report on the consultations to the NCC Governing Board, which we did. The board received our report and our very heartfelt request that the results of these consultations, especially the biblical consultation, be published, distributed, discussed in the churches, debated, challenged, and taught. The NCC then went through a painful leadership crisis, and the papers from our consultations were buried and ignored. To my knowledge, that was the first time in history that such a critical study of homosexuality and the Bible was presented and authorized at *that* level of church anywhere in the world. And yet the papers and findings remain suppressed to this day.

The leaders of mainline denominations and seminary professors from member churches of the NCC have *paid for* and *studied* this information about homosexuality for many years. Even conservative scholars like Richard Hays, previously from Yale and notoriously homophobic in his biblical interpretation (I don't know if he is or was in "the guild"), now admit that, for instance, the story of Sodom and Gomorrah is not and never was about homosexuality.[19] Yet the vast majority of Christians in and outside the churches of the NCC still believe outdated, erroneous, homophobic biblical interpretations. *The church leadership refuses to teach what it knows.* The violence and hatred perpetrated against gays and lesbians in our culture are silently—and sometimes not so silently—co-signed by the church. Church leadership knows that teaching the truth about homosexuality and the Bible will be controversial, difficult, and, at first, costly. The fear of controversy, of loss of money, and of criticism from the radical right keeps the truth locked up.

Bishop William Boyd Grove, chair of yet another NCC/MCC dialogue effort, said in one of our committee meetings that he thinks that homosexuality as an issue is like the little thread dangling from the lining of his coat. It doesn't look like such a big deal by itself, but he hears his wife saying, "Whatever you do, don't pull that thread!" Because, if he does, the whole lining of his coat will fall out! Church leaders instinctively know perhaps that the issue of homosexuality is only the most visible issue in a connected fabric of issues about human sexuality that the church cannot bear to see unravel.

Meanwhile, gays and lesbians continue to be vilified by conservatives in the United States and around the globe on the basis of outdated and thoroughly disputed homophobic interpretations of a few mostly obscure passages of Scripture. We at MCC do not have the power on our own to overturn this situation, at least not easily and not as quickly as it needs to happen. The leaders of the churches in the United States and around the world must take responsibility for what they know.

And I guess I want them to fix it because those of us at MCC, in all gay and lesbian spiritual and religious organizations, are *tired* of trying to fix it and of not being believed. We are sick of apologetics, of having to say over and over again why we believe the Bible doesn't condemn us as a special class of sinners. I want *them* to do it, because we have much more important, pressing, exciting, and enjoyable Bible reading and studying to do!

So let's get down to it: a lesbian hermeneutic of suspicion is a method of biblical interpretation that will make the connections among misogynist and homophobic and racist methods of biblical interpretation.

It will ask questions about those traditional homophobically interpreted passages that we call our "texts of terror." It will ask why certain passages have or have not been studied. It will examine biblical annotations and question the use of certain words and phrases. It will search biblical dictionaries and commentaries to identify trends in interpretations, cover-ups, omissions, and silences. Also, it will begin to *unsilence* silent biblical characters, and it will be free to engage in wild, bold, shameless speculation about gays and lesbians in the Bible.

A lesbian hermeneutic of suspicion cannot be myopic or be done in isolation. We have to understand the biblical interpretive methods of the religious right, and how they have been used against us. We have to understand how Catholics have used the Bible, and how liberation theology and African-American biblical scholarship help us to rescue the Bible from our oppressors.

Fundamentalists have gone through some changes in the past decades in how they preach and teach the "texts of terror" about gay men and lesbians. Today, their words might end up on a YouTube video that goes viral. Decades ago, LGBT people did not believe they could read the Bible for themselves and there was almost nothing published to support a positive reading of the Bible for gays and lesbians.

Several years ago my friend and spiritual writer, Chris Glaser, went undercover to an "ex-gay" conference in San Diego attended by 500 very sincere folks. Chris, in reporting about this in *Frontier* magazine and in conversations with me, said that there were no workshops about "Homosexuality and the Bible" at this conference. Instead, there were lots of testimonials from "healed gays" and seminars in bad psychology. Nothing on the *Bible?* Can it be that all the published critiques of traditional views of homosexuality and the Bible are becoming more difficult to refute? Have we begun to succeed in taking all the fun out of Bible study for homophobes?

I have noticed that both in articles by folks such as Richard Hays and in street-corner debates, the *soft sell* is very in. They've stopped talking about specific Bible passages (because we have credible responses now to Sodom and Gomorrah, Leviticus, Romans, and I Corinthians), and they're back to using pitiful statements like "God made Adam and Eve, not Adam and Steve." Well, true, God did make Adam and Eve. A charming heterosexual model couple! But one child put it beautifully, "Well, then who made Steve?"

Since then, the so-called "ex-gay" movement has stopped claiming that they can change sexual orientation—only behavior—and those changes only come with ongoing sacrifice. Lawsuits are in the courts charging misrepresentation, and laws to ban "reparative therapies" are under consideration. The main defense these days is freedom of religion—because people have a right to believe whatever falsehoods they want to in the name of religion.

Part of moving toward a positive lesbian and gay interpretation of the Bible means being willing to move ahead without the approval of fundamentalists or the NCC, and without converting them! No one is going to make this effort, this reclaiming of the Bible, easy for us. Nor can we make it comfortable for them—for fundamentalists, Methodist bishops, Baptist pastors, or even the Pope.

In 1987, Pope John Paul II visited the United States. One of the big events was to be a worship service in a stadium in Columbia, South Carolina. This was the *Protestant* showcase service and all the leaders of the NCC, plus Southern Baptists and others, were invited. All national Protestant church leaders were invited, and Rev. Troy Perry was on the list. We were never sure who made that decision in the National Conference of Catholic Bishops (what gay or gay-friendly person), but we were invited to participate in a procession of Protestant clergy into the stadium and to hear the Pope preach. Despite Troy's previous negative experiences with the NCC, he just couldn't resist this. He asked me to go with him.

It was the '80s and, as a lesbian pastor in a church that has its roots in the counterculture, I had an interesting history with just what *is* proper lesbian preacher attire! By 1987, I had gotten past the denim stage from the Seventies and had since been wearing pantsuits and clergy shirts. I had even bought a more *dressy* suit or two to wear to the NCC meetings, mostly so that I could blend in a little better. I figured I was "different" in enough ways obvious to all of us that I didn't need to make a statement with my clothing (like a lesbian flannel clergy shirt or something). However, the Eighties saw the revival of skirts and dresses in a big way (thanks to Ronald Reagan and the conservative wave), and this did make me feel a little awkward at times, and pressured to dress differently. With the invitation to worship with the Pope, it seemed as good a time as any to deal with the skirt thing.

By this time, I was pastor of MCC Los Angeles. Sweet, sharp-dresser Lloyd King, a member of the church, now in his eighties, gave me some money so I could dress myself. I was shocked at the prices of skirt suits and dresses since I had last bought them (probably high school). Still, I took the plunge and bought a suit, with a straight skirt and hemline below my knees. My wife, Paula, calls it my *nun* outfit.

Troy and I were both excited and nervous, not knowing what to expect at this event. We flew into Columbia, S.C., for an overnight. We saw no one we knew, and ate dinner together. Then I had to go to the drug store. And, unfortunately, I confided in him that wearing a skirt suit meant I had to wear pantyhose. And that I had not worn pantyhose in 15 years and that, when I wore them last, women shaved their legs. And I just didn't think I could wear pantyhose without shaving my legs! He thought that was hilarious and proceeded to include this in his repertoire of Fellowship folklore: *How Nancy shaved her legs for the Pope.*

Duly shorn, pantyhosed, and beskirted, I got in the car with Troy the next day as we drove to the stadium. When we got there, the rumor was that the Pope was late because there was a hurricane in Miami. We were herded into a large room, where eventually nearly all the 400 people in the procession were gathered. There were Catholics, Protestants, and Eastern Orthodox, clergy from the historic black churches, women and men of diverse religious backgrounds. We had vested, and then we ended up waiting for four hours in the early September South Carolina heat. Just *fabulous* for me in skirt, pantyhose, and brand new low heels.

To identify ourselves a little, Troy and I wore our buttons that said, "God is greater than AIDS." People would smile, introduce themselves sweetly, squint at our buttons, and read, "God is greater than *AIIIIIDS*," and turn away and quickly talk to someone else. There were a few friendly NCC folks, and a lot of unfriendly faces. The tension mounted as the temperature increased. I do not ever remember seeing so many police officers. The campus ROTC guarded us, assisted by the state police, local police, the FBI, and the Pope's own secret service. It was a madhouse.

Finally, the Pope arrived and the procession began. Some people were giving us the "how the hell did you get invited" looks. We processed in. Troy and I ended up on opposite sides of the football field, with the crowds watching above. I ended up surrounded by the Orthodox clergy, of course. As we walked in, someone unfurled a gay pride sign in the bleachers.

The service began with an opening prayer by a woman in a clerical collar. She then walked off the podium—by prior agreement, we learned. The Pope would not be on the same podium with a woman wearing a clerical collar!

Then came what was to be, for me, the highlight of the event, and the star of it was the Bible. The actress, Helen Hayes read the first lesson, from the Hebrew Scriptures. She read Ruth 1:16–17.

> But Ruth said, "Do not press me to leave you or to turn back from following you! Where you go, I will go; where you lodge, I will lodge;
>
> Your people shall be my people, and your God my God. Where you die, I will die—there will I be buried.
>
> May the Lord do thus and so to me, and more as well." (NRSV)

I was stunned. I had been sitting there thinking, "What the hell am I doing here?" Pope John Paul II was well loved, but he had not been exactly a leader in the area of justice for women, gays, and lesbians! In fact, for someone so well educated, who had spent his early life in the theater, he seemed the very paragon of sexual repression.

But along came Ruth and Naomi that day in South Carolina. It was like the Bible itself was speaking to me that day, reassuring me. The Bible was secretly overturning the moment, speaking for itself. The story of Ruth and Naomi was our text! It is the most profound statement of committed love between two human beings in the Bible, and it is said between two women (more about this later!). There was Helen Hayes, reading this beautiful statement ("Where you go, I will go; where you die, I will die."), right out there in front of the Pope, God, and everybody. It was a profound victory for lesbian hermeneutics.

Then the Pope himself read from the Gospel of Mark, chapter 3, verses 31–35.

> Then his mother and brothers came; and standing outside they sent to him and called him. A crowd was sitting around him; and they said to him, "Your mother and your brothers and sisters are outside, asking for you." And he replied, "Who are my mother and my brothers?" And looking at those who sat around him, he said, "Here are my mother and my brothers!

Whoever does the will of God is my brother and sister and mother." (NRSV)

Again, the choice seemed strange. First of all, this is one of the passages where it is mentioned that Jesus has brothers and sisters. In Catholic doctrine, which teaches the immaculate conception of Mary and her perpetual virginity, Jesus is said to be without brothers and sisters. Even modern Catholic translations like the Roman Catholic–sponsored Jerusalem Bible claim that the word for brothers and sisters may also have been used to mean "cousins." No Protestant commentaries say this. Secondly, I had always seen this text as one of Jesus' harshest statements against the idea that one's biological *family* relationships should define one's identity. In fact, Jesus *redefines family* as *those who do the will of God!*

The Pope then proceeded to use these two texts to preach a sermon that was essentially a campaign speech for *traditional family values*. He did have a really good subtext on the cross (he was, after all, in Baptist country). But most of the sermon was consumed by the "family values" stuff. Family values from whose tradition? Whose family? Both those Bible passages *critique* any "traditional" (really, modern!) understanding of family values. The Pope essentially ignored that in his interpretation or lack thereof.

And then he blessed the children. Later I would write a short piece for *The Christian Century* about it. He blessed a couple dozen children that day, at least 10 percent of whom were gay and lesbian. I was thankful that at least the Bible provided a *balance* that day, and I prayed that, when those children grew up, they would be included in the Pope's version of family. The Pope's sermon was so loaded with the "traditional family values" stuff that both Troy and I were expecting him to say something overtly homophobic. It never happened—and we hadn't planned what we would have done if he did. Would anyone on that big football field have taken notice—other than the FBI or the Pope's secret service?

The Pope had to rush off right away, being five or six hours behind schedule, so the promised reception line never happened. We went to the reception anyway and mingled with NCC leaders and Catholic bishops. A few of the bishops were extremely solicitous and knew right away who we were. One of them was well known to be actively homosexual.

We showed up and made some people wonderfully uncomfortable. The Holy Spirit showed up in the reading of scriptures that told us we can be at home wherever we are.

Others have blazed this trail toward our home and our true selves. Any hermeneutic that scrutinizes the Bible to sort out the harmful and liberating messages and interpretations must understand that African Americans broke open the scriptures in an unprecedented way when they challenged the use of scripture to reinforce slavery and prejudice.

Over the decades, the gay and lesbian movement in the United States has been largely *perceived* as a white male movement. Some of this is due to racism in the media that defers to stories about white people, and it is at least in part because LGBT white people, like other white people, are enculturated with sexism and white racism. Sexism means women's concerns get minimized, and racism means too many white people believe we have an apparent divine right to rule, whether we acknowledge this or not.

This means that black gays, lesbians, and bisexual and transgender people have had to walk a tightrope. To come out has often meant leaving home and family and culture behind. It has meant coming out into a white-dominated gay movement and having to work for change on both the outside and the inside of your movement. It has meant that black LGBT people have often been asked to educate white leaders rather than being free to reach out to the black community. Racism in the United States has made overcoming homophobia in the black community more complex. In addition, the particular ways in which homophobia is related to sexism and the way that sexism and racism affect each other have made it hard for us to engage in dialogue about sexuality across racial lines.

Today, groups like the Fellowship of Affirming Ministries, the Global Justice Institute, and the National Black Justice Coalition are making history by declaring clearly that African Americans have good reason to support their LGBT family and community members. When the NAACP and President Obama came out in support of marriage equality, African Americans who had been looking for public leadership to reinforce their changing opinions found it and began to be more comfortable with their own stand for justice. Black pastors and scholars were vital in the sweeping wins for President Obama and all four state-level ballot measures in the 2012 election.

Diversity has been an emphasis in the movement now for decades. Many know that oppressions cannot be equated. Heterosexism and racism are not identical. When African-American politicians and church leaders do not support LGBT rights, some charge that "the oppressed have become the oppressors." Many of us know, it is not that simple.

First of all, African Americans do not have the power to reinforce their prejudices in our culture the way white people still do. Although anyone can have prejudices against persons of other races, in our world today, especially in the United States, white people are more likely to have the power, wealth, and resources to make our prejudices count for something. White racism, as some have defined it, is the combination of personal prejudice with institutional privilege.

Second, there are many white gays and lesbians who have not really dealt at all with our racism (or sexism). We should have the same horror at ourselves as we understand our own *oppression* based on sexual orientation and gender identity but don't lift a finger to resist the massive imprisonment of people of color or the economic disparities and personal prejudice that perpetuate racism, sexism, and classism. Why do we not also see ourselves as "the oppressed becoming the oppressors"?

I have also heard or seen African-American leaders act shocked when gay and lesbian people talk about oppression. This is made worse when the stereotype of gays and lesbians as a wealthy white minority is proffered by gay activists. The economic oppression of gays and of blacks is not equivalent, but it is also necessary to challenge the "white wealthy" stereotype of gays and lesbians.

With this in mind, I want to acknowledge and engage with the work that African-American biblical scholars and historians of African-American biblical interpretation have done, as integral to a queer hermeneutic of the Bible—and integral to any group that has experienced the Bible as being interpreted to oppress them rather than to free them.

Michael Cartwright shows that African-American suspicion of the slave owners' Bible was core to their engagement with the Bible:

> Part of what distinguishes the African-American Christian tradition of biblical interpretation from other interpretative traditions is that reading—or literacy in the broadest sense—and the interpretative problems posed for African Americans by racist interpretations of Christian Scripture have been linked to one another *almost from the moment African Americans were taken from Africa as slaves.* Slaves were taught that the Bible "talked" to the master, but on those occasions when African-American

slaves attempted to get the Bible to talk to them, they encountered silence. Given the fact that the slaves had been taught that "the Bible said" God had cursed them, it is no wonder that enslaved Africans concluded that the Bible would not speak to them because of the color of their skin.[20]

Tired of listening to Euro-American preachers who appeared to read "obey your masters" on every page of the Bible, African-American slaves rejected their masters' interpretation of the Bible and the "slave ideology" by which it was legitimated. Instead, they gathered in "secret meetings" where they sang and danced and, in effect, reconstructed the Bible in relation to the spirituals and conversion narratives of the slave community. The fact that these gatherings were illegal, and that they were also occasions in which slaves taught one another to read, simply underlines the degree to which the very act of reading the Bible was a threat to the slavocracy.

Given this racist ideology based on a few excerpts, it is amazing that more African Americans have not rejected the Bible. But, however tempting it may have been to rid themselves of the icon of their oppression, African-American Christians rejected this kind of "monologic" solution in favor of reading the whole Bible with its core message of freedom and love. At the same time, "the black churches have never hesitated to *disavow* any interpretation of Scripture that would attempt to legitimate racism, slavery, or any other form of human bondage." Based on this historical assessment, some scholars have been tempted to make formal claims about the text of the Bible: "there is no sacred Scriptures for blacks apart from the hermeneutic principles by which they are received and transmitted."[21]

Over the years, many black authors (starting with W. E. B. Du Bois), sociologists, and linguists have written about the "double consciousness" that existed in the minds of black slaves in the United States, as they heard about and then eventually read the Bible for themselves. They wrote about how slaves heard and used the text to speak with a "double voice" about their experience. James Cone, in *The Spirituals and the Blues*,[22] wrote about how the words to many spirituals conveyed double meanings. Hymns that praised heaven were really about praising the freedom that could take place by traveling north. Many spirituals are filled with images of crossing over, crossing rivers, traveling on trains, being bound for glory, about destinations and a happier future, about the suffering and struggles of this life. "There's a meeting here tonight" was more about secret antislavery meetings and plans to escape than about church services. The slave had to develop this double consciousness: the public, open language he or she used in the presence of the white slave owners; and the private, almost double-entendre language that could even be spoken in the slave owners' presence without them understanding. This was an encoded language, shrouding feeling and intention.

The Bible, as literature that expressed some powerful ideas to the slaves who bothered with it, became part of this double-voiced vocabulary.

Because most slave owners thought it was a good idea to "Christianize slaves" (in order to be able to control them more, with God on their side and the Bible to keep slaves in their place), slaves knew that "talking Bible talk" was relatively acceptable and safe.

But the Bible had and has its own agenda. It contains the stories of deliverance from slavery and oppression, expressed in spiritual terms such as "My Lord delivered Daniel, why not *everyone?*" The Bible spoke to the hearts of slaves its own unrepentant, uncontrollable revolutionary message: "Let my people go!"

After the Civil War, much of the African-American focus on the Bible was apologetic, especially in refuting the racist interpretations of the story of Ham in Genesis and overturning the "Bible justifies slavery" interpretations of Philemon and other New Testament passages. More recent African-American biblical scholarship sees no need to deconstruct the slave and curse texts because the constructive tasks of describing how black culture—jazz, religion, visual arts, writing, intelligentsia, survival, and so much more—runs through the veins of the body of what we call American religion and culture.

Some LGBT people have compared being in the closet to slavery in a way that does not take into account the *real differences* in these two experiences. This is similar to the way people today use the term *closet* generically to mean "anything kept secret or hidden." Sometimes that usage feels as though it trivializes the painful experience of gay and lesbian oppression. So, too, comparing the closet with slavery can result in trivializing the horror of being owned by another human being, held captive against your will, beaten or raped at whim, wrenched from your family, lynched, or murdered, with no recourse for justice.

Slavery is not just another form of oppression, and the closet is not just another *secret*. For gay and lesbian people, living in the closet, having to lie and cover up our sexuality, has been soul killing and has often resulted in suicide, isolation, loneliness, and despair. It has been the source of enormous emotional, psychological, and spiritual pain. It has also been the cause of physical pain and discrimination. Gay people in the closet are more likely to engage in high-risk sexual encounters and may be targets for extortion or other threats. They are at more risk for gay bashing and job discrimination.

Slavery, as an imperfect analogy, however, can help us understand our situation and our relationship to the biblical text. Gay and lesbian people, too, have had to have a kind of *double consciousness*, a secret vocabulary, an encoded language for public and private use. We, too, have tried to live in this double consciousness in a heterosexually dominated culture. We, too, have our "texts of terror" that have been used to justify the homophobia of the church and culture.

It was an NCC official who first said in 1992 that the issue of homosexuality and the church is the "most divisive issue in the church since slavery." Then it became impossible not to use that analogy and take it to its logical conclusion:

Imagine if there had been a church council in the United States just prior to the Civil War. The church council consisted of free and slaveholding churches. For the "sake of unity," this council elected never to discuss the issue of slavery, for fear of offending each other's sensibilities. Most of the "free churches" did have African-American members, but these members were not in a position of power or leadership. In a few cases, African Americans from free churches even represented their churches as delegates, but only with the clear understanding that they would never bring up the issue of slavery and that they would be as discreet as possible and would not be offensive to delegates from slaveholding churches. Blacks who were light-skinned or who could pass as white were preferred.

All is well until the day that the church of mostly freed slaves applied for membership. These were slaves of all hues, many with visible scars of body and soul. This "church of freed slaves" is a young church, still getting organized but growing by leaps and bounds as people begin to find their way to freedom. This is not a "quiet" church. They are loud and proud, angry and full of joy in their newfound freedom. They come to witness to the powerful, miraculous, redeeming love of the God of Jesus Christ, who has saved them and set them free. They want the whole church to hear of the wonderful things God is doing. How folks are healing from the devastating effects of slavery. How they are providing marriage ceremonies for men and women who had not been permitted to marry while enslaved. How God is healing their children and elders. How they provided for each other with "burial societies" because white people's mortuaries and cemeteries wouldn't accept them. How they were helping each other adjust to the new world of freedom, which still contained so much racism.

They came to this council to witness and to be included. They did so not only for themselves but for all the slaves they still knew in captivity, people who were held as slaves by some of these Christian folks. They spoke for the ones who did not dare to speak.

There was no way this council could admit a church of freed slaves without freeing their own slaves, without having to make a commitment *that slavery was* wrong. So the council tried to ignore the church of freed slaves. They formed committees to study the issue, they tabled it endlessly, hoping the little church would have enough other issues to deal with that it would get discouraged and drop its request for inclusion.

This analogy has helped me spiritually and emotionally to work through some of the insanity that occurred in MCC's relationship to the National Council of Churches. As a church of "freed slaves," MCC is a living ecumenical witness to what a community for LGBT people and our families looks like. We terrify closeted gays and lesbians; we anger liberals who want us to love them for their private support while publicly betraying us; and we exasperate those conservatives who are convinced we can't be Christians when we pray and sing and testify to God's love for our community.

In November of 1992, in Cleveland, Ohio, at the General Board meeting, the NCC voted narrowly not to accept MCC as an observer to the NCC—even though we were already observers to the World Council of Churches. At the time, even non-Christian organizations were given observer status by the Council. Unitarians (which include Christians, but do not have a Trinitarian Christian doctrine), a Muslim group, and a Jewish organization all were observers of the NCC. There were no criteria for observer status.

We actually applied to be observers as a semi-graceful way of ending a long and painful (disgraceful at times) "dialogue to nowhere" that ended up being just a prolonged stalling tactic for not dealing with our membership application. We simply had no idea that asking to end all the silliness by settling for observer status would be controversial. But they debated for five hours about it, and then they voted no. No officer of the NCC spoke in our favor. From the floor, Dr. Paul Sherry, head of the United Church of Christ, along with the Methodists and a few others, pleaded for rationality. But to no avail. One young lesbian, a visitor (not from MCC) said, quite sincerely, "Even if you (the NCC) thought MCC was *of the devil*, wouldn't you want them to observe you so they could learn how real Christians act?"

Since that time, we left that organization to minister to our members and mobilize for equality in community after community. MCC congregations are often the community centers where there is no LGBT center. One of our members recently served as the president of the North Carolina Council of Churches. MCC is in 40 countries. Our leaders are on the cutting edge of efforts for marriage equality. We have joined forces with the Fellowship of Affirming Ministries to form the Global Justice Institute for international justice work from the perspective of religion.

In the faith world, the Unitarian Universalists and the United Church of Christ have been joined by the Presbyterian Church (U.S.A.), the Evangelical Lutheran Church in America, and the Episcopal Church in having no obstacles to ordaining lesbian or gay people. Transgender people in all traditions are telling their proud and powerful stories.

Sadly, many traditions such as United Methodists and Orthodox Christians have become more entrenched than ever. The United Methodists global body took a vote on "whether grace was available to all people" and barely passed it because of heterosexism. Orthodox leaders in Eastern Europe and Russia have supported some of the most repressive laws anywhere. African Christians of Anglican, Catholic, and Evangelical traditions are promoting virulent forms of homophobia in the name of Christianity. U.S. evangelists who are losing the battle in the nation are turning to places like Uganda, where their anti-gay agenda has been well-received.

These deadly theologies claim they are based on the Bible. But I offer you another way: the way of Jesus, who picked up a scroll and read the Prophet Isaiah to the elders in his hometown and said, "Today this Scripture has been fulfilled in your hearing" (Luke 4:21). I warn you, they promptly tried to kill him—but all it took was a look into their eyes and they let him go, knowing that their rush to judgment had more than fulfilled the words of Isaiah.

Be brave. Know that the scriptures were meant for you to read, interpret, and apply to your queer lives. Join me in my extravagant welcome to this open book—to detoxify and demystify, to speculate and embody what Jesus did, to read the scripture and transform the world!

3 • Detoxing the "Texts Of Terror"

Part of the difficult work of a lesbian hermeneutic of suspicion is to tackle head-on those "texts of terror" that reinforce the irrational biases of church and society.

Phyllis Trible, in her book *Texts of Terror,* takes on a very difficult area of feminist biblical interpretation: How can certain passages of Scripture that seem to justify violence and dehumanization of women be included in the canon? Are all parts of Scripture equally valuable or valid? How do we discover and discern the "canon within the canon"? And what is our stance toward obviously misogynist stories in the Bible?

The texts in the Bible that have terrorized gays and lesbians have been used, accurately or not, to justify the homophobia of the church and culture. Judges, legislators, and governors in our country *still* quote the Bible when justifying the denial of civil or human rights for gays and lesbians.

How can a group of people claim to be a legitimate minority group if the Bible says that God disapproves of or even hates them? People who may never dust off or read a Bible are just *sure* that it says bad things about gays and lesbians.

When I teach people at MCC about homosexuality and the Bible, I help them learn how to stand up to those who would make such claims. The first thing I suggest they do is to ask the question: "Where? Show me *where* the Bible mentions gay men or lesbians and condemns us." In about two-thirds of the cases, this will stump them right off the bat. We live in a very biblically illiterate society. However, if you are dealing with people who know the Bible (and fundamentalists are more likely to know chapters and verses), they will at least know about the story of Sodom and Gomorrah, and that it's in Genesis.

What is really enjoyable is for those of us who are gay or lesbian to be able to recite the passages that are our texts of terror *for* our *opponents*. It really throws them off! They can't believe that anyone who is gay has ever opened a Bible. And that we would not be afraid to know these passages and to discuss them. I've had fundamentalists *insist* on looking at my Bible to see if it's a "real" Bible or a special *gay* edition. (I wish!)

Interestingly enough, the New Revised Standard Version of the Bible includes the most amazing annotation as a comment on Sirach 22:3, which reads: "It is a disgrace to be the father of an undisciplined son, and the birth of a daughter is a loss." The annotation says of verse 3b, "This reflects the *misogyny* of the age."[23]

It is a remarkable thing that the word *misogyny* actually appears in the text of the annotated Bible. Before I die, I would love to see an annotation to at least one of the texts of terror for gay men and lesbians that says, "This passage and its traditional interpretation reflect the homophobia of the age(s)." It will happen.

I do not want to spend time in this book going over the *explanations* about how to reinterpret these texts of terror. I would simply refer you to the best material available.[24]

Instead, what I would like to do is to take on the New Revised Standard Version of the Bible and the other biblical study aids and critique their handling of the texts of terror. This, for me, gets to some of the heart of the politics of biblical interpretation as it affects gay men and lesbians in the present.

I believe it was crucial for MCC to be in study and dialogue with the National Council of Churches for many years, despite their treatment of us, because they own *the copyright* to the New Revised Standard Version of the Bible (NRSV). This is very important because this is a highly influential version of the Bible, and it grows out of the more liberal tradition of biblical criticism.

If positive changes are to be made in the biblical text or its interpretation, they will most likely appear in this version first. Also, because the owners of the NRSV have a reputation for using the best information available, including modern critical tools and methods, and because they have access to the emerging critique of the texts of terror, they have *more responsibility* to reflect these critiques in the translation and annotation, even if doing so is politically unpopular.

If we use the logic of Elisabeth Schussler-Fiorenza's "feminist hermeneutic of suspicion," then what is *omitted* from a text or commentary may be as important, if not more important, as what is included. Both the presence and the absence of points of view and voices of characters—as well as the commentary on them—are important. The owners, publishers, and scholars who produced the NRSV know that a single word omitted, changed, or added to a text, or annotation to a text, is very, very important.

According to Dr. Shannon Clarkson, linguistics scholar and member of the NRSV translation committee, thousands of male pronouns were removed in the translation for the New Revised Standard Version because they were not part of the original Hebrew or Greek from the Bible. The earlier Revised Standard Version translators saw no problem with adding male pronouns.

So, to some degree, previously marginalized groups (women/ people of color) found their way into the power structures that produce new Bibles. It took longer for gay and lesbian theologians and biblical scholars to have an impact on scholarship, but it is happening. Today at the American Academy of Religion meetings, queer studies are increasingly present.

The Revised Standard Version of the Bible was published in sections between the late 1940s and early 1960s and is the first version to use the relatively modern word "homosexual." The New Revised Standard Version of the Bible was better translated, but the commentaries were very disappointing. What may seem like very minor inclusions, changes, or omissions from the text or annotations are the strange and sad politics of biblical translation and interpretation for gays and lesbians.

Today, in the 3rd edition of the New Oxford Bible, the scholarship is catching up to the commentary. When the 3rd edition came out, Troy Perry wrote:

> I'm excited to share with you today one of the most important theological breakthroughs in the 33-year history of Metropolitan Community Churches. ... The world-renowned biblical scholars who prepared *The New Oxford Annotated Bible* have adopted a great deal of MCC's own scholarship and theology: There is no biblical condemnation of homosexuality—only prohibitions against its misuse, just as there is no biblical blanket condemnation of heterosexuality, only prohibitions against misuse of that gift.

Although the third edition of the New Oxford Bible made great strides, old habits die hard.

The Treatment of the Sodom Story in the Bible Texts and Commentaries

The basic story line is that God sends two angels to destroy the "twin cities" of Sodom and Gomorrah because of some *great wickedness*. The city is the home of Abraham's cousin Lot, and, in a previous chapter, Abraham intercedes with God about the fate of Sodom and Gomorrah for the sake of Lot and his family. The result of that intercession is that, rather than just blow the city up outright, God sends the two angels to Lot to warn him and help him and his family escape.

In the process, the people of the city hear about the two strange visitors and threaten them with violence (possibly with rape). The angels blind the violent citizens of Sodom and Gomorrah and help Lot's family escape. *Then* they blow up the city.

This story has an interesting history of interpretation, first documented by D. S. Bailey 40 years ago.[25] Basically, the story of Sodom and Gomorrah was not associated with homosexuality at all until the Jewish philosopher and biblical commentator Philo of Alexandria wrote his commentary in the first century (CE). Philo devoted many pages to enumerating and elaborating on the precise nature of the sins of Sodom and Gomorrah based on his own vivid imagination—and nothing more. His fantasy was apparently so compelling and thorough that it was picked up by the early church fathers and simply passed on for two millennia without being challenged. This could only happen because of homophobia. Basically, Genesis 19 was not studied very much for nearly two millennia, and, because Philo's interpretation reinforced cultural prejudice against homosexuals, it seemed plausible. His explanations included graphic descriptions of homosexual acts (none of which are specifically referred to in Genesis 19) and accusations of bestiality (totally without any basis in Genesis 19).

The only possible link to homosexuality is the use of the verb *yadah*, translated "to know" (Genesis 19:5). This verb is used in only a few instances in the Bible to refer euphemistically to sexual intercourse. When the wicked folk of Sodom and Gomorrah want Lot to send out his guests that they may "know" them, this *may* have been a euphemistic reference to an "indecent proposal," or the threat of rape. Obviously, the people's intentions were bad, whether or not violence of a sexual nature was the plan. And if these were men threatening to rape men, it had nothing to do with love and orientation—it was a way that *heterosexual* men humiliated other men, especially in the context of conquest.

To appease the attackers, Lot offers them his *daughters!* Lot knew this was about sexual violence, and the sexism of his time allowed him to offer his daughters rather than the men in his protection. The sexism of our time allows most readers to skim over the gross betrayal of his own daughters—and the silence of their mother.

How do readers make the leap from condemning male *rape* (not a sexual act, as we now know, but an act of violence) to claiming that therefore *all* homosexual acts and relationships are wrong? One only makes that leap if one is homophobic!

So, how does the NRSV incorporate the research on homosexuality and the Bible that began 40 years ago with D. S. Bailey?

What is most interesting are the annotations in the NRSV. The text remains essentially translated as it always has been, which is really not a problem! But the annotators say the following:

> 19:1–38: *The destruction of Sodom and Gomorrah* impressed itself deeply on later generations as an example of God's total judgment upon appalling wickedness (Deut 29.23; Isa 1:9; Jer 49:18; Am 4:11). 1: *Two angels, see* 18:2–8n. 4–11: Compare the crime of Gibeah (Judg 19:22–30). The episode is told to illustrate the sexual excesses of the Canaanites. 5: *Know* refers to sexual relations (v. 8), here homosexual (sodomy).[26]

The Bible is the best interpreter of the Bible, and the cross-references here (Deuteronomy and so on) are very interesting. In *none* of these references to Sodom and Gomorrah is there any remote reference to sexuality or homosexuality. There are, however, references to idolatry. In addition, one very important reference is omitted: Ezekiel 16:46–58. Only if you look up the annotations to Isaiah 1:9 and 10 will you find a cross-reference to Ezekiel. *This passage from Ezekiel is very important because it is the only passage in all of the Hebrew Scriptures that gives a definition of the sins of Sodom and Gomorrah!* One of the important things to note, in reading this passage, is that sexual impropriety, prostitution, and "lewdness" were repeatedly employed by the prophets as metaphors of Israel's unfaithfulness to God.

The passage from Ezekiel documents Jerusalem's *religious* apostasy and uses the metaphor of a "faithless bride" to do so:

> Have you not committed lewdness, beyond all our abominations?

> ...Your elder sister is Samaria, who lived with her daughters to the north of you; and your younger sister, who lived to the south of you, is Sodom, with her daughters. You [Jerusalem] not only followed their ways and acted according to their abominations; within a very little time you were more corrupt than they in all your ways. As I live, says the Lord God, your sister Sodom and her daughters have not done as you and your daughters have done. *This was the guilt of your sister Sodom: she and her daughters had pride, excess of food, and prosperous ease, but did not aid the poor and needy. They were haughty, and did abominable things before me; therefore I removed them when I saw it.* Ezekiel 16:46–58

Several things are apparent in this passage and in the verses that follow: in no way is the "sin of Sodom" associated with sexual behavior of any kind. The term *abomination* was a very specific word that referred to idolatry, not literally to *sexual* sins. Sexuality is used as a *metaphor* for spiritual apostasy, but only as a metaphor. There is no suggestion that sexual misconduct was the basis for God's judgment against Sodom and for her consequent destruction. In addition, Ezekiel makes the point later on in this section of chapter 6 that God says, "I will restore the fortunes" of Samaria, Sodom, and Jerusalem. In any mention of Sodom and Gomorrah, I have never heard one biblical commentary ever mention that (1) Ezekiel claims that the sins of Jerusalem were worse than the sins of Sodom (were all of them homosexuals, too?) and (2) that Ezekiel prophesies the *restoration* of Sodom, along with others.

Why does the NRSV ignore Ezekiel 16 in its annotations to Genesis 19? I believe, in part, because Ezekiel 16 does not support the contention that this story is in any way about homosexuality.

It was particularly damaging that the annotation to verse 5 of Genesis 19 (already quoted), used the word *homosexuality* when 40 years ago D. S. Bailey and others after him pointed out that this passage is *not* about sexual relations (homosexual or heterosexual) but about violence (and possibly rape). This is not a minor flaw. Perpetuating the association of homosexual sex with the word *sodomy* was extremely irresponsible.

Importantly, this was *new* to the 1991 version; it is not found in the old RSV. The word *sodomy* in English was used in English jurisprudence to describe the homosexual act of male anal intercourse and bestiality *based on the erroneous interpretation of Sodom and Gomorrah that the Jewish philosopher Philo and his successors in the church taught.* Thus, the problem is circular: the word *sodomy* comes into the English language based on erroneous homophobic exegesis, and then the English word is used in the annotation of the NRSV to reinforce the association of homosexuality with Sodom and Gomorrah!

The consequences are that, for the duration of the life of this commentary on the Bible, gay and lesbian people will continue to be associated with this violent, negative story and will have this association used against us in the courts, the legislatures, the churches, and on the streets. It becomes a contributing factor toward gay bashing, having our children taken from us, bans on adoption and marriage, and all forms of injustice toward gays and lesbians.

The more recent third edition of *The New Oxford Annotated Bible* takes a step in the right direction. Here are the NRSV scripture reference, the second edition annotation paragraph, and the third edition annotation paragraph:

> *Genesis 19:5–8:* "And they called to Lot, 'Where are the men who came to you tonight? Bring them out to us, so that we may know them.' Lot went out of the door to the men, shut the door after him, and said, 'I beg you, my brothers, do not act so wickedly.'"

> **Second Edition:** The destruction of Sodom and Gomorrah impressed itself deeply upon later generations as an example of God's total judgment upon appalling wickedness, ... The episode is told to illustrate the sexual excesses of Canaanites. 5: *Know* refers to sexual relations, here homosexual ("sodomy"). 8: Once guests had eaten in his house, Lot felt he had to

obey the law of oriental hospitality, which guaranteed protection. Thus his proposal to hand over his daughters showed his determination to put first his obligation as a host.

Third Edition: The destruction of Sodom and Gomorrah was a prominent example in Israelite tradition of God's total judgment. As in the case of 18:1–8, the main issue here is hospitality to secretly divine visitors. Here, however, the sanctity of hospitality is threatened by *the men of the city* who wish to rape (*know*) the guests. Though disapproval of male homosexuality is assumed here, the primary point of this text is how this threat by the townspeople violates the value of hospitality.... As a result of his protection of his guests, he [Lot], like Noah, "finds favor" with God and he and his household are rescued out of destruction.

The third edition removes the blatantly biased equation of homosexuality with "sodomy" but fails to remove the inherent equation of homosexuality with the evil of Sodom.

In contrast, the new *Anchor Bible Dictionary* has a five-page article on Sodom and Gomorrah.[27] *The word homosexuality does not appear in this article.* It states, "The transgressions of Sodom's inhabitants consist in sexual debauchery [is that a synonym for rape?], human hubris, and violation of the (law of) hospitality."[28] The article does *mention* the history of interpretation, including references by rabbinical teachers to the ways in which the people of Sodom and Gomorrah "reversed" the laws of nature. And, in those times, the "laws of nature" referred to the *human moral law,* not to the scientific concept of nature as we moderns think of it. Those reversals of the "laws of nature" included the folklore about Sodom and Gomorrah that their laws *were calculated to do injury to the poor and the needy.* They were a sort of ancient "Town without Pity."

As good and more fair-minded as this article is, it is curious to me that the author does not refer to D. S. Bailey's book in the extensive bibliography. And, though I am appreciative that the author appears to be the first extensive commentator on Genesis 19 who does not perpetuate the association with homosexuality, I would have preferred it if he had *mentioned* that 2,000-year association and why he decided *not* to perpetuate it. Silence, in this case, is better than slander, but it is not quite golden. It becomes the interpretation that dares not speak its name!

Sodom and Gibeah

There is a similar story of rape in Judges 19:22–30. It is remarkable in two ways: how incredibly similar the story is to the story of Sodom and Gomorrah, and how differently the story is treated in its translation, annotations, and the history of its interpretation.

The *men of the city* of Gibeah are called a "perverse lot" in the NRSV, and as in the Sodom and Gomorrah story, they pound on the door of a man and demand to have access to a male guest (a Levite) in order to molest him. The interpreters in this case translate the same verb, *yadah* (to know) as "intercourse" ("so that we may have intercourse with him").

The annotation to these verses reads: "To forestall his own *rape* by the men of Gibeah, the Levite gives them his concubine, who they rape all night long. She is either dead or simply cannot move in the morning. He doesn't take her in to help her heal; he puts her on his donkey and, when he arrives home, he cuts her body into parts and sends it to the twelve tribes of Israel to foment war."[29]

It is fascinating to me that nowhere in the text or annotations does it suggest that these men of Gibeah were homosexuals or sodomites. Why not? It also uses the correct term for their intention toward the Levite and action toward the concubine: rape. Why isn't the word *rape* used in the annotation to interpret the Sodom and Gomorrah story?

Also, this story is practically unknown in the popular mind, unlike the story of Sodom and Gomorrah, although it is equally or more horrifying. In this story, the concubine is raped all night long and is in fact *murdered* and *dismembered*. The *threatened* rape of the two (male) angels in the story of Sodom and Gomorrah has excited more outrage (and homophobia) for 2,000 years than the actual rape and murder of this woman. This is misogynist biblical interpretation.

One last word before we leave Sodom and Gomorrah (and, unlike Lot's wife, let's not look back!): Jesus does make a reference to these "twin cities" in Matthew 10:1–16. In this passage, Jesus is sending out the disciples to preach the good news, "cure the sick, raise the dead, cleanse the lepers, and cast out demons" (Matt. 10:8). He gives them instructions on how they are to travel and how to deal with their reception in the towns and villages they enter. To those who do not receive Jesus' disciples with hospitality, he gives the following warning: "Truly I tell you, it will be more tolerable for the land of Sodom and Gomorrah on the day of judgment than for that town" (Matt. 10:15). Jesus uses the famous story of Sodom and Gomorrah not to inveigh against any sexuality but to warn against inhospitality toward those he has sent.

The only other significant reference to Sodom and Gomorrah in the New Testament is in Jude: "Likewise, Sodom and Gomorrah and the surrounding cities, which in the same manners as they, indulged in sexual immorality and pursued unnatural lust, serve as an example by undergoing a punishment of eternal fire" (Jude 7).

Well, there it is, you say! *"Pursued unnatural lust"*—a reference to Sodom and Gomorrah that is implying homosexuality. Not so! The passage is in the context of the discussion of fallen angels, and the note on the words "pursued unnatural lust" says, "Gk: went after other flesh." In other words, an alternate translation of the Greek words *is:* "went after other flesh." The strangers who came to Sodom and Gomorrah were not men but angels. Verse 8 in Jude actually continues this thought: "Yet in the same way these dreamers also defile the flesh, reject authority, and slander the glorious ones." The annotation in the NRSV states: "In spite of warnings, the heretics defy authority, revile *angels* [apparently those angels who are God's servants], and live licentiously." It's the threatened rape of angels, not homosexuality, that has Jude upset.

Other Texts of Terror

If we turn to the *Anchor Bible Dictionary,* it has the following notations under the heading "Homosexuality: See prostitution; punishments and crimes; Romans, Epistle to the; and sex and sexuality."

What this means is that the *actual word* "homosexuality" *does not appear in its original Hebrew or Greek equivalent in the whole Bible!*

Part of the reason for that is that the word *homosexual,* in English, did not come into existence until the 19th century. Any English translation of the Bible before that will not contain the word *homosexual,* and the NRSV only contains the word *homosexuality* in the annotations and in very misleading ways.

Was there a Greek or Hebrew word that is the equivalent of our English word *homosexual?* I don't know of one Hebrew word that describes us as a whole class of people, but there is such a word in Greek: *homophilia.* This describes not just sexual behavior but a relationship. *The word "homophilia" does not appear anywhere in the Greek New Testament.*

So, let's see what the *Anchor Bible Dictionary* has to say in these secondary references to homosexuality:

1. **Prostitution:** In the two articles that appear in the *Anchor Bible Dictionary* on prostitution, the word *homosexuality is* not used. However, there is some discussion about the existence or not of male cult prostitution and how that might have been related to fertility cults, or how it might or might not have found its way into the life and culture of ancient Israel. Nothing helpful at all about homosexuality per se.

2. **Romans, Epistle to the:** There is a long article in the *Anchor Bible Dictionary* about Romans, but nowhere in it could I find the word *homosexual*.[30] It does have a short paragraph on Romans 1:18–3:30, which includes the second most famous "text of terror" for gay and lesbian people, Romans 1:18–27, which reads:

> For the wrath of God is revealed from heaven against all ungodliness and wickedness of those who by their wickedness suppress the truth. For what can be known about God is plain to them because God has shown it to them. Ever since the creation of the world his [sic] eternal power and divine nature, invisible though they are, have been understood and seen throughout the things he has made. So they are without excuse; for though they knew God, they did not honor him as God or give thanks to him, but they became futile in their thinking, and their senseless minds were darkened. Claiming to be wise, they became fools; and they exchanged the glory of the immortal God for images resembling a mortal human being or birds or four-footed animals or reptiles.
>
> Therefore God gave them up in the lusts of their hearts to impurity, to the degrading of their bodies among themselves, because they exchanged the truth of God for a lie and worshipped and served the creature rather than the Creator, who is blessed forever! Amen. For this reason God gave them up to degrading passions. Their women exchanged natural intercourse for unnatural, and in the same way also the men, giving up natural intercourse with women, were consumed with passion for one another. Men committed shameless acts with men and received in their own persons the due penalty for their error.

In the commentary, it says that Paul is demonstrating that both Gentiles and Jews "deserve divine condemnation and punishment when judged on the basis of their 'works.'" The author of the article says that the word *them* in verses 23 and 25 refers to "Gentiles" (not homosexuals): "The Gentiles, though they 'knew God' (Romans 1:21a) did not give God the reverence and thanksgiving due him [sic] (1:21b). Instead, they became idolaters (1:21a–23), the result of which was all manner of sordid behavior that violates the divine will (1:24–31) and makes them worthy of divine condemnation" (1:32).[31] Is this why the *Anchor Bible Dictionary* makes the cross-reference to "homosexuality"? "All manner of sordid behavior"? Is Paul saying that this is a uniquely Gentile "sin"? Is it only about homosexuality? Homosexuality *under cover* of idolatry (and not other homosexual behavior)? *All manner* of sexual behavior practiced in the context of idolatrous worship and living? This is never clarified for us in the Bible or in the commentaries.

3. **Sex and Sexuality:** This fascinating article by Tikva Frymer-Kenskey says some very helpful things, first about the metaphysics of sexuality:

> In these laws of social control over sexuality and its consequences, we can detect a respect for the power of sexual attraction. Controlled and confined within the marital system, it reinforced the social order. Allowed free reign, it might destroy social arrangements and threaten the existence of civilization. The metaphysics of sex, however, only finds explicit statement once in the Bible: "for love is as fierce as death, passion as mighty as Sheol, its darts are darts of fire, a blazing flame. Vast floods cannot quench love, nor rivers drown it" (Song of Songs 8:6–7).
>
> . . . There is no sexuality in the divine sphere. God, usually envisioned as male in gender, is not phallic; God does not represent male virility, and is never imagined below the waist.... This absence of sex from the divine realm is accompanied by a separation of sexuality from the realm of the holy.... Previous theories about Canaanite orgiastic rites or pagan sexual fertility rituals cannot be substantiated. The separation of sexuality from the realm of the holy should *not* be seen as a polemic against pagan religion but as a result of the lack of sexuality in the

conception of the divine. This created a vacuum in thinking about sex, one that was ultimately replaced by the negative Greek ideas about women and sexuality which entered Israel in the Hellenistic period, dumping it on Jewish thought. Also, of course, the Christian church came into being during that *Hellenistic period* in the life of Judaism.[32]

This research also undercuts the notion that Jewish ideas about sexuality and homosexuality were a result of a *revulsion* toward pagan fertility-cult prostitution.

The comments in the same article about homosexuality are the only explicit ones in the entire *Anchor Bible Dictionary* and are as follows:

> Israel's intense interest in regulating sexual behavior is an aspect of its concern to prevent intermingling between individuals and groups who should be separate.
>
> . . .Like sex with a daughter-in-law, sex with an animal is also called *tebel*, "(improper) mixing." Homosexual intercourse is not labeled *tebel*, but the extreme prohibition of homosexuality by the death penalty (Lev 29:13, Cf 18:22) , *not inherited from any other ANE [Ancient Near East] laws*, is best explained as a desire to keep the categories of "male" and "female" intact. Anything that blurs the lines, such as cross-dressing, is also prohibited (Deut 22:5). Lesbian interaction, however, is not mentioned, possibly because it did not result in true physical "union" (by male entry). The biblical view of creation is one of organization and structure; collapsing the categories of existence is a return to chaos. See punishments and crimes.[33]

The second edition of *The Oxford Annotated Bible* says, "Also omitted is any prohibition against homosexual acts between women, though the framers of the laws may not have envisaged that such even existed"[34]

Fascinating! Homosexuality (male) is an ironic exception to the rule of the prohibition against *intermingling*. In this case, the idea is to keep the genders "intact" by making sure the sexes intermingle! This, of course, would make sense in any patriarchal culture (which brings up the question, does it make sense in a non-patriarchal culture?). The penalty had to be severe because of course there were always a certain percentage of people who were naturally inclined not to stay "intact"! This desire to keep the male and female roles intact is, of course, the basis of sex-role stereotyping, the purpose of which is to keep women in their place. It is also interesting that "lesbianism" *doesn't count* because a penis is not involved. "True physical *union*" is equated with *male (penile) entry*.

That reminds me of a story. Rev. Elder Jean White, former pastor of MCC South London, talks about viewing a TV show about homosexuality with her mother a few years after she had come out. Jean's mother finally turned to her and said, "Well, you can't really call what you women do together *sex,* dear, can you?"

Queen Victoria refused to sign a law prohibiting lesbian sexual relationships because she simply couldn't be persuaded that women did such things, and, if they did, how could it possibly count if there was no penis involved?

So, homosexuality would "collapse the categories of existence" and "return us to chaos," "destroy social arrangements," and "threaten the existence of civilization"! This is *cosmic* homophobia. This is a primal fear excited by the existence of homosexuals. And what kind of "organization and structure," what kind of "social arrangements" and "civilization," are we talking about? Patriarchal!

I do have to say that I appreciate the honesty of the writer in documenting how the importance of lesbianism was negated in ancient cultures, although it makes me furious. I could certainly have wished for some theological or political insights about how this ignoring of lesbianism was related to the undervaluing of women in general. It really hurts not even to rate a minor biblical condemnation in Leviticus or elsewhere! Lesbian invisibility is about *female invisibility* in the Bible—and everywhere else.

Also, I find the constant pairing of bestiality and homosexuality to be really annoying, but these vile comparisons are the stock and trade of opponents—and sometimes our friends try to use such comparisons in misguided efforts.

I remember a tense moment in one of our NCC dialogues during which an NCC staff member was commenting on the proposal of one mainline U.S. denomination to refuse to baptize gay and lesbian people. Because this church practices infant baptism, we were all a bit mystified about how the identification would be made (just refuse to baptize every tenth child?). Nevertheless, she said, "If you will pardon the comparison, what about murderers? The church doesn't say it won't baptize murderers." In one sense, I agree—point well taken.

In another sense, "What the heck do you mean, 'pardon the comparison'?" No, I will *not* pardon or accept the comparison, thank you very much. When homophobic, patriarchal culture rules, love between two people of the same gender is *worse* than murder. When that translates into a culture like ours that is addicted to violence, that *finds it sexy,* we must rethink what we mean by perversion.

Here's a really interesting bit of biblical trivia, besides: Exodus 20:13 is one of the Ten Commandments: "Thou shalt not kill." The Bible critiquing the Bible! Leviticus 20:13 says to kill queers; Exodus 20:13 says don't kill—point that out to fundamentalists![35]

There are lots of actions that were deserving of the death penalty in Leviticus: cursing your father or mother (20:9); adultery (20:10); being a medium or a wizard (20:27); prostituting yourself, if you are the daughter of a priest (20:2); sacrificing your children to the God Molech (20:2). I think of the bumper sticker I have seen that says, "Kill a Queer for Christ." You *never* see one that says, "Kill an Adulterer for Christ," or "Curse your parents, go to the chair!" It would be preposterous to say, "Hang all psychic readers and advisers," but this does point out that gays and lesbians get selectively targeted for Levitical battering.

Back to the NRSV and how it treats us gay folks. There is no annotation on Leviticus 18:22, the first prohibition against homosexual (male) relations. Perhaps we should be grateful about that! But the annotation for Romans 1:24, 26–28 states, "They [the annotations don't say this, but 'they' means Gentiles] violated their true nature, becoming involved in terrible and destructive perversions; God has let the process of death work itself out. 26–27: See 1 Cor. 6:9n."[36] In this commentary, the word *homosexual* is not used, but there is an unnecessary reference to another "text of terror" whose only connection is that Paul is also the author. The language describing the "sin" in 1 Corinthians 6:9 has nothing in common linguistically with Romans 1:18–27, except in the history of biased interpretation, and in the prejudiced minds of the commentators.

The translation and annotation of 1 Corinthians 6:9 are perhaps the most disturbing, because they ironically are the only comments that take into account any of the scholarship of the last 40 years. They take it into account and then blow it!

So, 1 Corinthians 6:9 states, "Do you not know that wrongdoers will not inherit the kingdom of God? Do not be deceived! Fornicators, idolaters, adulterers, male prostitutes, sodomites, thieves, the greedy, drunkards, revilers, robbers—none of these will inherit the kingdom of God" (NRSV).

For me, the most grievous and painful error in this translation is the use of the term *sodomite*. It is the first time of which I am aware that an English translation of the Bible has used this term—which we have already established is a gross misusage, based on an erroneous interpretation of the Sodom and Gomorrah story! So now, for the first time in the history of the English translation of the Bible, the word *sodomy* is legitimized as being *about* homosexuality. The words *male prostitutes* and *sodomites* are English translations for two Greek words: *malakoi* and *arsenokoiti*. Much has been written about these two words. They do not appear with much frequency in the Greek language or lexicons, so translators have always had to guess at their meaning. In many cases, the two words were combined and translated "homosexual" (as in the previous version of the RSV). It is possible that these words did refer to a specific kind of homosexual behavior, *which may or may not have been practiced by homophiles* or the social equivalent of what we today call gay men. In any case, the annotation to 1 Corinthians 6:9 does nothing to clarify it: "6:9: Male prostitutes, young men or boys in a pederastic relationship; sodomites, the older homosexual; see Romans 1:26–27; 1 Tim. 1:10; possibly 1 Cor. 11:4–7 is pertinent."

First of all, the opinion that these two words mean "a young boy prostitute" and "an older homosexual" john (or heterosexual john who is seeking homosexual sex) is a *guess*. The annotation should say that. Secondly, the equation of *sodomite* with "older homosexual" is misleading and damaging. This annotation now leads us to the last "text of terror," but, before we go there, what about the cross-reference to 1 Corinthians 11:4–7?

As we turn to that passage, we see that the context is one of the more troublesome texts for women. It describes a "divine" descending hierarchy from Christ to man to woman:

> Any man who prays or prophesies with something on his head disgraces his head, but any woman who prays or prophesies with her head unveiled disgraces her head—it is one and the same thing as having her head shaved. For if a woman will not

veil herself, then she should cut off her hair; but if it is disgraceful for a woman to have her hair cut off or to be shaved, she should wear a veil. For a man ought not to have his head veiled, since he is the image and reflection of God; but woman is the reflection of man. (1 Corinthians 11:4–7).

Well, I'm confused. What about you? Among other things, we realize that this is why Paul has never been very popular with feminists!

What do the annotators have to say about this passage? More about the "misogyny of the age"? Nope. Here's what is said: "Reflecting the first-century culture, a man dishonors Christ by worshiping with his head covered; a woman dishonors both her husband and Christ by worshiping otherwise. 4–7a: Confusion of gender, see 6:9n."[37]

So, the implication (it's implied, not stated!) is that this is some weird first-century custom, and just don't worry your heads (male or female) about it. However, the *deadly* reference is this "gender confusion" inserted into the annotation. The implication is that this "male prostitution/older homosexual pederastic sodomy" referred to in 1 Corinthians 6:9 is about gender confusion. Well, I think *they* are confused. This comment assumes a theory of psychology *not in evidence,* namely that homosexuality is tantamount to *gender* or *gender-role confusion.* Frankly, that is outdated, bad psychology and irresponsible Scripture "scholarship."

Last but not, I'm afraid, least, we have 1 Timothy 1:10: "fornicators, sodomites, slave traders, liars, perjurers, and whatever else is contrary to the sound teaching" (NRSV). There is no comment on this verse in the annotations to the NRSV.

I do like the appearance of the words *slave traders, liars,* and *perjurers* in this verse, however. All who sought to justify slavery conveniently forgot this verse, I guess. Also, the church has lied and perjured itself in the ways in which it has dealt or not dealt with sexism, slavery, racism, and homosexuality. So I guess we're all in the same boat. In actuality, of course, the only time 1 Timothy 1:10 is ever dredged up is in the service of gay bashing.

So, I would give the translators and annotators of the New Revised Standard Version a low grade on their scholarship and sensitivity to the emerging critical issues related to homosexuality and the Bible. And, although it appears *The Oxford Annotated Bible* authors are now paying more attention to current scholarship on texts that have placed burdens on LGBT people, they have need to work harder. They need to disclaim and discredit interpretations that are the proof texting for condemnation and violence against gay, lesbian, and any gender non-conforming person.

My friend Chris Glaser shared a quotation from an unnamed source one year on his Christmas card that said, "Jesus, save us from some of your followers."

My focus has been on the NRSV because of its standing in the academic world. You would be correct to assume that more conservative translations do even more harm. The New International Version of the Bible, for instance, translated 1 Corinthians 6:9 as "male prostitutes or homosexual offenders"—much worse than the NRSV. In 1 Timothy 1:10, the same word is translated "perverts," with no explanation for the different translation.

In the *Vines Expository Dictionary of New Testament Words*, the Greek word *arsenokoiti* appears with no definition. But the Greek word *malakos* has an interesting, somewhat balanced exposition:

> *Malakos: soft, soft* to the touch (Lat. *mollis,* English mollify, emollient, etc. are from the same root), is used (a) of raiment, Matt. 11:8 (twice); Luke 7:25; (b) metaphorically, in a bad sense, 1 Cor. 6:9, "effeminate," not simply of a male who practices forms of lewdness, but persons in general, who are guilty of abdication to sins of the flesh, voluptuous.[38]

I think it is really a far cry from this Greek word to the statement that all homosexuals and all homosexual behavior are repugnant to God. But, all you voluptuous people, watch out!

4 • Outing the Sodomite

Until D. S. Bailey published *Homosexuality and the Western Christian Tradition* in 1955, the ancient philosopher and biblical commentator Philo was the single voice that had defined the "sin of Sodom." With the advent of a gay and lesbian religious movement in the late Sixties, Bailey's writings were "discovered" by gay folks, and a new hermeneutic of the story of Sodom and Gomorrah, found in Genesis 19, began.

For nearly two millennia, the lie that the story of Sodom and Gomorrah was a story about homosexuality (or bestiality, or anal or oral sex, or *queer sex* of any kind) prevailed and validated homo-hatred in the Western world and every place in the world where Christianity had gotten a foothold. If God hates queers enough to blow up two cities because of them, then homophobic hatred is justified and maybe even holy! The story of Genesis 19 became a virtual religious *license to kill* those whom God deemed unacceptable. But, with the onset of the gay and lesbian religious movement, we began to *read* D. S. Bailey and to write and teach ourselves about this tragedy of biblical interpretation.

Part of the tragedy has been that Philo's interpretation was allowed to stand unchallenged because homophobia and homo-hatred meant that scholars did not want to study Genesis 19 or other passages that purportedly dealt with homosexuality. D. S. Bailey went beyond a *superficial* examination of Genesis 19 and exposed the problems in Philo's original interpretation. We began to educate ourselves and to attempt to educate other Christians. In the Seventies, there were literally a handful of other books and pamphlets (mostly produced by MCC and Evangelicals Concerned) that began to tell of this new interpretation of Sodom and Gomorrah. Today, even conservative theologians know that Genesis 19 does not support wholesale condemnation of homosexuality.[39] The biblical sources for proof-texting (quoting Bible verses out of context to prove a point) homophobia are dwindling, thank God.

The problem is, of course, that the most biblically illiterate people in the world, who barely know any of the 23rd Psalm or even two of the Ten Commandments, are just *sure* that the Bible and God condemn homosexuality—and they vote.

When our MCC church was located on Washington Boulevard in Los Angeles, we were across the street from a gas station and minimart. There were several men who lived on the street, most of them addicts, who washed car windows at that location for spare change. Our church had a kind of symbiotic community with these guys, some of whom I came to know by name if they were able to talk at all. Church members were a good source of spare change, and some of these men actually watched out for the church building. One was a young, handsome man named John. He was smart and manipulative and well spoken, and he always addressed me respectfully. (He'd probably grown up in church.) One day, while I was trying to prevent him from washing my windows (the car was actually newly washed for a change!), he said, "Can I ask you something?"

"Sure."

He then told me that he'd seen two women leaving the church walking arm in arm or holding hands. Maybe it was the first time John realized that there were gay people involved in the church; I'm not sure. He said that this bothered him, them walking down the street like that because wasn't it *against the Bible*?

Now, mind you, this man was a crack addict and a panhandler who spends half his life in and out of the county jail. He lies, steals, and is throwing his life away because he is sick with addiction. But he was morally shocked and offended by two lesbians he had seen touching each other in public in a way that is acceptable for heterosexual partners or spouses to show affection! Not only that, but he believed —he *knew* —that the Bible supported him in this disapproval! So I gave John a very short version of "Homosexuality and the Bible." I also told him I was a lesbian, and his eyes widened. He looked over his shoulder to see if any of his buddies were watching him. Then he spoke confessionally, and let me know that he had had homosexual sexual experiences. He was clearly conflicted about this. Somehow, deep inside of what is left of this man's personality and heart, he is sure God will forgive him everything else, *but not this.* I shifted the conversation to say to him, "John, I just hope that, whenever you have sex, you have safe sex and use a condom—do you understand what I mean?"

"Yes, ma'am," he said sheepishly.

I let him know that there were free condoms available in the men's rest room in the church. With that, I got in my car and left him to sort it out for himself.

For days I thought about that incredible conversation. How did homosexuality get to be *the* unpardonable sin, worse than addiction (self-murder), stealing, or lying? Is it the depth to which gay and lesbian sexuality and lifestyle threaten "heteropatriarchy"? Is the *ultimate* crime or sin against God the overthrowing (or even just the providing of an alternative to) the domination by men of women through sexuality? So that a poor, young black male crack user who long ceased caring about his own life, who has long since given up hope for anything but another day of survival and using, can *still* be shocked and frightened by observing two women breaking the alleged sexual norms of his day—and frightened by his own secret desires and sexual feelings? *How amazing!*

Such internalized homophobia can create great tragedy. On Sunday, June 24, 1973, MCC New Orleans was meeting on the second floor of a bar. More than 50 people were listening to pianist David Gary's music and discussing an upcoming MCC fundraiser for the local Crippled Children's Hospital. At 7:56 p.m., a buzzer from downstairs sounded. The bartender opened the door to find the staircase engulfed in flames. One group went out of the back exit to the roof and climbed down from another building's roof to the ground floor. Dozens were left inside the second-floor club. Some attempted to squeeze through barred windows in order to escape. Several escaped, but returned to bring out more patrons from the fire— only to die. The fire lasted 16 minutes; 32 people died.

Coverage of the fire by local and national news outlets minimized the fact that LGBT patrons had constituted the majority of the victims—or that it was a faith group meeting there—while editorials and talk radio jockeys made light of the event. Only one clergyperson, Reverend William P. Richardson of the St. George's Episcopal Church, agreed to hold a small prayer service for the victims on June 25. Some 80 people attended the event, and Richardson was rebuked by his bishop and his mailbox filled with hate mail.

A week later, two memorial services were held at a Unitarian Church and at St. Mark's United Methodist Church, headed by Louisiana's United Methodist Bishop Finis Crutchfield (whose identity as a bisexual man came out at his death) and led by MCC founder Rev. Troy Perry, who had flown in from Los Angeles. Several families did not even step forward to claim the bodies of the deceased. A few anonymous individuals stepped forward and paid for the three unknown men's burials, and they were buried with an identified victim named Ferris LeBlanc in a mass grave at Holt Cemetery.

A man who frequented the bar was convicted of pouring lighter fluid in the entry and setting it ablaze. He escaped from the police, and, even though he was seen in New Orleans bars again, he was never taken into custody again. Like the daughters in the story of Lot and the concubine in the story of Gibeah, the mass murderer and New Orleans considered some people expendable.

The Sin of Sodom and Gibeah

The sin of Sodom and Gomorrah was the sin of *inhospitality to strangers*. What queer theologies have pointed out is that the church of Jesus Christ is guilty of sodomy—deadly inhospitality—especially to gays and lesbians, "Inhospitality" hardly describes the "sin of Sodom." It is a euphemism for gross cruelty. Linking the Sodom and Gomorrah story to the story of the murder of the concubine in Gibeah (Judges 22),[40] *the sin of Sodom, is nothing less than the sin of ethnic and sexual violence.*

When we look at the Sodom text, we should ask, why were these angels targeted for rape? In Gibeah, were all foreigners raped if they stayed too long? Or were the angels targeted because they broke gender expectations? Were they perceived as a loving same-sex couple! If so, the two gay *angels* are the potential *victims* in the story, not heterosexuals. The man with his concubine also had a servant with him. Historically, servitude has often included sexual obligations. Why didn't the man send out his servant rather than his concubine?

Rape, we have come to learn, is not a sexual crime or sin primarily. Rape is a means of physical, mental, and spiritual domination. It is an act of ruthless power: the annihilation of the "other." In both stories, the father is perfectly willing to send out his own daughters. At Gibeah, the father offered to send out his daughter who was the concubine—as well as a second daughter who was still a virgin—all to protect the men who appeared to be the intended victims.

As I look at the stories of Sodom and Gibeah, both the "other" and the "female" are objectified to the point of being expendable. Physical brutality and domination becomes the tool to dehumanize, silence, obliterate. This action is not personal, it is systematic, calculated. It is the family value of domination through violence whose intent is power or profit or both. This is the sin of Sodom and Gibeah.

Sodom and Gibeah are ancient stories of *ethnic cleansing* that we see replicated in our age in Nazi Germany, in the genocide of the Armenian people, in Bosnia, and in South Africa. Today, LGBT people in more than 70 countries around the world can be imprisoned or executed for being who they are. Russia and Nigeria, among others, have recently passed gag-order laws that make even talking about LGBT people and our rights a crime punishable by imprisonment.

When the MCC congregation in Charlotte, North Carolina, bought a small building in a suburban area 20 years ago, the neighbors found out that there were "queers" on their street. During worship service, people appearing to be adults and claiming to be Christians stood outside the church and turned on power saws and power mowers to disturb a small group of mostly (not exclusively) gay and lesbian Christians who were praying and singing hymns. This is not just inhospitality, although it is surely that; it is violent, threatening, and vulgar. Men with power tools in hand (how can we miss *that* metaphor?) stalked a small MCC church outside the door and windows of a sanctuary. It is a scene highly suggestive of sexual violence. In an updated way, it very nearly replicates the scene outside of Lot's house in Genesis 19.

Inside the church (like Lot's house), there were humans, and perhaps angels, who made sure no one was hurt physically. This happened in the year before MCC was admitted to the North Carolina Council of Churches. This gave encouragement to the council to publicly confront the homophobia of MCC's neighbors, which they did, and this helped defuse the ongoing violence.

There is another twist in the story. In many ways, the Council of Churches played the same role as Lot and his family in the story of Sodom and Gomorrah. They are basically good people, minding their own business, who live in an extremely violent culture, where sodomy—now understood as sexual and racial violence—is rampant. In the Genesis 19 story, two angels (of the same sex!) appear at Lot's door. He has to decide whether or not to take them in. And what will be the consequences of offering them hospitality? Who was Lot afraid of? Who was peering in at their window, spreading gossip about whom Lot let in that night? Who began fueling the chain saws, getting the crosses ready to burn in North Carolina? The crowd at Lot's door that night is the *same* faceless, cowardly crowd that has lynched black men and burned their homes, raped and killed black women, and that rapes women and bashes gays in our streets every day, in North Carolina, and all over this country.

In 2011, the North Carolina Council of Churches elected a lay leader from the Metropolitan Community Churches as its president. The recent campaign to prevent the constitutional banning of marriage for loving same-sex couples failed, but North Carolinians will never be the same. They have been outed as a state moving toward equality.

Sodomy was the sin of the Virginia Court of Appeals when, in 1993, the court cruelly removed Sharron Bottoms's two-year-old from her home because she was a lesbian. Ironically, the child was awarded to Sharon's mother.[41] One woman responded in the *Los Angeles Times:* "The court in its wisdom has taken from a lesbian her adorable two-year-old and turned the child over to the heterosexual grandmother who bore and raised the lesbian daughter to begin with. Can we talk?"[42]

Sodomites have persecuted Brenda and Wanda Henson in Ovett, Mississippi, for more than 20 years. These two women have been trying to live their quiet rural lifestyle, run a camp called Camp Sister Spirit for feminists, and help women escape from violent homes. In 1993, the *Los Angeles Times* reported that "they have been subjected to anonymous phone calls, threatening letters, jeers, and random gunfire from their neighbors. A bomb has been exploded in front of their gate, and a dead dog was found draped over their mailbox. The climate of intimidation has intensified with two meetings led by Baptist ministers to raise money to force the Hensons out of their former pig farm."[43]

It is sad to report that the violence has continued since then. Those North Carolina women are no more harmful than the two angels who appeared on Lot's doorstep. But somewhere deep in the consciousness of the Sodomites, they know that these angels are bringing warnings, challenges of changes needed. Their presence tests whether the people of the city are *righteous or not.* This is a test that sodomites, by definition, always seem to fail.

The *Times* also reported that "Paul Walley, a lawyer advising the groups persecuting the Hensons, explained that 'the area is a conservative religious community that has a standard based on biblical morality. Residents of Camp Sister Spirit reject that standard and have a radical agenda that would seek to change our way of life.' Their biblical moral precedent is apparently not the injunction of Jesus of Nazareth to *love thy neighbor.*"[44] On the contrary, it was this mandate to *love thy neighbor* that was so troubling for the religious leaders of Jesus' day—and is rarely understood today.

Sadly, racist, sexist and heterosexist violence is still a fact of life. The National Coalition of Anti-Violence Projects 2011 report stated that, while hate violence has decreased, the number of hate murders against the LGBT community has increased—and, of those, 87 percent were people of color. Our transgender brothers and sisters are more likely to live in poverty or die violent deaths than any other group. These crimes are often marked by "overkill," violence to the body long after death and mutilation.

What is it about hatred of the other, those who are different in race, ethnicity, or sexuality, that inspires such, brutal murderous rage? Why is it that rape and mutilation and torture so often accompany such murders? One thinks of the ethnic cleansing in Bosnia, which included so much rape and torture. It also brings to mind racist murders and lynching and their long history (which continues today) in the United States. Rituals of Klansmen have included *dressing* up for the occasion!

In 1998, James Byrd was tortured and murdered by unapologetic racists. In the same year, Matthew Shepard was hung on a split-rail fence, pistol-whipped, and left to die.

It also seems to me that this kind of sadistic sexual or ethnic violence serves a more sinister political purpose, but those who benefit from this purpose are not usually the ones visibly doing the acting out. The participants are influenced and driven by forces behind the scenes that manipulate mass culture, that incite the rage of those who have *just enough* power to be able to subdue those *just below* them.

The story of the origins of the Ku Klux Klan in our country is the *classic* example of the way in which wealthy, powerful politicians and businessmen convinced poor and working class whites in the South that their class solidarity with blacks was worth trading in for "white privilege." It is a tragic story about how people who are under economic stress can be convinced that the only way for them to improve their lot is to make sure that someone is made to feel inferior to them.

This is the same story today of the growth of right-wing militia groups in our country, who are frustrated by the gradual decreases in the standard of living, and who want to blame that on racial/ethnic minorities, "liberals," "feminazis," and, of course, homosexuals.

They come to believe that murderous rage is justified—not unlike the murderous rage of the Sodomites or the Gibeahites. So, just what is God's response to all of this? In the story of Gibeah, God seems absent or silent. In the story of Sodom, God seems angry *at* the murderous, would-be rapists. Perhaps in these texts of terror, God turns to humanity and is asking what our response is. Are we silent? Are we angry? Do we care?

5 • Outing the Bible: Our Queer Texts

In the face of this destruction we must rebuild our lives. As Christians, we must construct new interpretations of the scriptures. In this task, I want to go too far! We've come a long way in a few years in the queer community. However, in terms of boldly and comfortably claiming our presence in the Bible, we haven't gone far enough.

My experience is that, as far as the world and the ecumenical movement are concerned, we have already gone too far just by virtue of showing up. Even in the LGBT movement for equality, there is a tendency to push LGBT clergy and faith leaders out of the picture now that some of our straight allies are speaking out. They seem more acceptable to the voting public.

Being the first open lesbian in many settings has taught me a lot about how provocative our mere existence seems to be. Minority groups are often perceived as more threatening or "larger than life" to the dominant group. The dominant group has all kinds of fantasies about what *they* will do if *they* outnumber or overpower *us*.

Early in the life of MCC, women were a small minority. If there were ten men and two women in a room, most men thought of it as *pretty well balanced!* I remember when Troy Perry took my wife Paula and me to a popular gay bar in Hollywood after a big MCC event in about 1980. Troy wanted especially to impress Paula, and he told her that the bar was about "fifty-fifty" (meaning 50 percent men and 50 percent women). When we got there, there were hundreds of sweating, discoing gay men, two straight women, one possible lesbian, and a drag queen. Troy was flustered and apologetic, and Paula never let him forget it. I watched Troy struggle to understand if this was just an *unusual* night at the bar or if his perception had somehow really been that far off. He never forgot that lesson about perception.

Often, in efforts at dialogue between MCC and others, we've been in settings where gays and lesbians were a small percentage of the total group, but were perceived as "overpowering" by the heterosexuals. This is the same kind of phenomenon that often happens in racial contexts.

I used to joke with NCC leaders about our meeting locations. During the planning process for structured consultations, we would have two meetings per year in an airport hotel in Newark, New Jersey. Most of the NCC people came from the East—actually from Manhattan. MCC headquarters are in Los Angeles. I told them that meeting in New Jersey was just *their* idea of "meeting us halfway"! (Hey, it worked for them!)

We have always had to travel further in our consciousness, patience and forbearance, energy, money, and effort to participate in the larger culture. So have all marginalized people.

In this chapter, I am not willing to meet anyone halfway. So, come along if you dare. You've read the warning label!

I don't want to apologize or be subtle. I don't even want to have to be very careful. A bold, proactive reading of the Bible has offered me and others new life as lesbians, gays, and bisexuals. When we are willing to read the Bible from *below,* from our vantage point, the Bible comes alive with new relevance.

What if we just *assumed* that lesbians, gay men, bisexuals, and transgender people were *always* in the Bible? What if we just accepted the fact that our counterparts followed Moses and Miriam in the Exodus, wandered in the wilderness, and walked with Jesus by the Sea of Galilee? We were there! Even when we were silent or closeted about our sexuality. Even if many people in those ancient cultures repressed their sexuality or never expressed it (which is doubtful!), we were there.

It is time boldly to "liberate" some biblical queer characters and stories from ancient closets. It may seem unfair to "out" these defenseless biblical characters, but I'm tired of being fair. Centuries of defamation and silence in biblical commentaries and reference books have not been fair. A passionate search for biblical truth about sexuality must be undertaken. It is time for shameless, wild speculation about the Bible and about *human* as well as *"homo"* sexuality. Our speculation will not destroy the Bible. If we are wrong about some of our speculation, no one will die. In fact, some people who thought they deserved to die just for being gay or lesbian may actually begin to believe that there is hope for them—and live.

Biblical scholars have always found a place for speculation and imagination when reading the Bible. Thousands of books and stories have been written that expand on or amplify the Bible. These writers do not claim to be infallible, and neither do I. They imagined, wrote, and speculated out of their deep love and involvement with the characters and messages of the Bible. All of these are a part of my motivation, too, and I, too, am motivated by the needs of my own community.

The Jewish tradition of *midrash* is very relevant here. Rabbis and other Jewish writers have always claimed the right to *expand* on a given text. To give voice to those who do not speak; to imagine, in a textually consistent way, what they would have said. Allowing the silences to speak is one of the powerful methods of a feminist hermeneutic of the Bible.

It is time for us to let the gay and lesbian and bisexual characters and inferences have voice, life, and dimension.

Does the Bible actually include references to or stories about gays and lesbians *consistent with what historians and anthropologists know about sexuality during biblical times?* The answer is yes. Some stories are incontrovertible. Others are compellingly gay or lesbian. And there are other characters, stories, and images that are curiously suggestive of same-sex relationships and gender non-conformity. All of these can empower LGBT people to embrace the Bible joyfully.

LGBT people have long had the "opportunity" to develop our capacity for forgiveness. We are one of the few minority groups (the only one) whose members do not necessarily share their minority status with their families. We are rejected, punished, and excluded by our families and churches, as well as by the larger society. In order to live, we have had to learn how to let go, grieve, survive, and forgive.

In order to embrace the Bible joyfully, many people will have to *forgive* the Bible, as well as forgive those who have used it to hurt and punish and ostracize them.

I've seen gay and lesbian people open a Bible fearfully, as if it would physically hurt them to read it. They have *Biblephobia*. For those of us who grew up thinking that the Bible was a source of spiritual authority, the word of God, and the story of Jesus' love, the experience of being verbally abused with a Bible was devastating. It was an experience of betrayal. It was no longer safe to open a Bible, to read it, or even, sometimes, to own one. And along with this pain came the loss of all the *good stuff* that the Bible had provided.

For other queer people, the Bible was never particularly inviting. It was mysterious, intimidating, old-fashioned, male-dominated, and hard to read, so they never tried. So, what many gay and lesbian people have heard of the Bible is someone else's interpretation. Warmed-over, leftover, biased views of the Bible are a constant undercurrent in American popular culture.

I remember the moment when a person training to be a deacon at MCC Los Angeles suddenly realized that the Bible had a story line. She had always thought of the Bible as a set of instructions, "pearls of wisdom," lists of laws, and so on. Nowhere had she ever learned or heard that there was a *story* that connected all the books and characters of the Bible. I used diagrams, charts, and very *compressed* lectures to help people get the *big, sweeping picture* of the Bible's story line. When she realized this, she was delighted! It was exciting—there was actually a story here that could somehow relate to our story.

Overcoming the fear and hurt and learning to forgive are necessary elements in a queer appropriation of the Bible. Obviously, not everyone will want to do it.

As I was preparing to preach a sermon series on "Outing the Bible" at MCC Los Angeles, some of our members took flyers into the street of West Hollywood. The flyers said:

God doesn't approve of gay and lesbian lifestyles, right?

THAT'S BULL!

Come and hear ...

At first, some of the people receiving the flyers thought that members of our group were fundamentalists—until they read it carefully! However, even some of the gay men and lesbians who knew that our group came from MCC reacted with hostility just to the mention of the words *God* and *Bible*. People from our church were cursed as gays and lesbians on the street. Some ripped up flyers and shouted, "F— the Bible!"

Every time something like this happens, I try to teach MCC Los Angeles people not to take it personally and, instead, to utter a prayer.

First of all, a person who would react that way is hurt and enraged, possibly a preacher's kid or a survivor of some authoritarian, homophobic religious abuse. Also, we can say a prayer of thanksgiving. As hard as this is to say, because I also love the Bible, I believe it is better for these people to say, "F—the Bible" than to *believe the crap* other people tell them about the Bible. And, even though they rejected the message today, their angry reaction ensures that they will never forget that they encountered a gay or lesbian person who somehow feels there is still something of value in a relationship with the Bible. Perhaps at some future date, when they are ready or are more needy than angry, they may remember and reach out and be able to claim or reclaim a healthy relationship to whatever religious tradition or text is theirs—or make their peace with it and move on.

Then there are those who pause and say, "Tell me more." These are the folks who want to liberate the Bible. The story MCC has to offer is a powerful one. Rev. Freda Smith, the first woman ordained in MCC, has said many times that MCC is the "most exciting church since the Book of Acts." Sometimes we identify very strongly with the intensity, challenges, and dilemmas of the first Christian communities.

That desire to be compared with the early church typifies a very *American* view of church. American sects, as well as many earlier Reformation churches, often have seen themselves as recreations of the "primitive church," and MCC is *not* the first church to make this kind of claim for itself. The longing to recapture that experience has its own history in the life of the Christian church. We long for a "primeval" Christian experience that predates the time when the church and the remains of the Roman Empire merged.

Unlikely as this may seem to some people, there are some ways in which MCC shares some of the features of this early church—although we must always be aware of over-romanticizing ourselves or that early church.

In the early days of MCC, we never called ourselves a denomination. Denominations were what we had left behind—those narrow dogmas, doctrines, divisions, parochial loyalties. We were an *ecumenical fellowship.* In many ways, we are a post-denominational denomination. The term *post-denominational* has been in vogue in church circles for some time now. The issues, doctrines, and practices that brought about denominational divisions do not matter to most people. That trend had made MCC's ecumenism understandable and attractive to many people.

On the other hand, MCC looks a lot like a denomination in that we do have a style of organization that includes a modified form of hierarchy;

we do have a very simple statement of faith; and we, like other denominations, have a headquarters and endless meetings! So, we've been a little ambivalent about our status as a denomination. Partly, our identification as a denomination is a way in which we are trying to appear less sectarian, less marginalized, and more "mainstream."

Like the early church, MCC is young in the formation of its theology, its style of polity and worship. We were created not out of a theological dispute per se or as a break-off from one *particular* denomination or branch of the church family tree. Instead, we were *called out* from all denominations out of a desperate need, representing all races, classes, walks of life, ages, and lifestyles. Sometimes people in MCC can hardly believe whom they are sitting next to in church. It is one of the most difficult aspects of MCC to manage at times, and one of the most inspiring and attractive (to some!).

We meet where we can—sometimes in office buildings, other churches, funeral homes, bars, and private homes. Some own their own buildings, others still struggle to pay the rent and a part-time salary for a pastor. Most have limited resources and a devoted core of committed leaders and members. Over the years, dozens of churches have been burned or vandalized. We've experienced persecution, so we "recognize" ourselves in the Book of Acts.

There has also been a sense of the miraculous that reminds me of the first church. Troy Perry's book *Don't Be Afraid Anymore* documents this wonderfully.

The first-century church existed within the context of a common language, Hellenistic culture, and safe travel. All these helped the church to grow. MCC is a church that has grown up in the fertile context of a great, global gay and lesbian community in the midst of its worldwide awakening. The Book of Acts is an account of an early church that attempted to preach and embody an "unhindered Gospel" (Acts 28:31). MCC today is a powerful *ecclesiastical* movement whose first audience is the gay and lesbian community, most in need of an unhindered Gospel.

Reading the Bible and preaching at MCC means that I am forever comparing our experience to the experience of the early church. In the story of Peter and the Roman centurion Cornelius (a Gentile), Peter (a Jew) is given a divine vision from God accompanied by a revelation that "God shows no partiality, but in every nation anyone who fears God and does what is right is acceptable to God" (Acts 10:34–35).

The Peter and Cornelius story is just ripe for gay and lesbian exegesis! Peter grew up in a Gentile-phobic culture. And for good reason. In the Hebrew Scriptures, every time the Jews ran into trouble, it was because of their association with Gentiles (and Gentile gods and religious practices). So, the easiest way to handle this problem was just not to associate with them: Don't eat their food, don't eat with them, don't marry them. However, there were also prophetic voices in Judaism that expressed countervailing opinions: David's great-great-grandmother Ruth was a Moabite! Jonah, the reluctant prophet, is chastised by God for his unwillingness to preach salvation to the Ninevites. Isaiah prophesied of a time when Gentiles would be included in the true worshipping community (Isaiah 56). The earliest Christians—all Jews—just assumed that one had to be a Jew in order to be a Christian. Nothing else seemed remotely conceivable. In fact, it was probably *heretical* and *blasphemous* to think otherwise!

Then Peter has this "rooftop vision" one afternoon. A huge sheet of all kinds of animals, clean and unclean (kosher and non-kosher), is spread out in front of Peter, and God tells him to *kill and eat*. This happens three times. The thought of eating non-kosher animals is repulsive to Peter. It violates every cultural and religious sensibility he has been raised with. He has been taught to believe that to do so would be to dishonor God and break God's law.

And now he hears *God's voice* saying, "Do not call anything impure that God has made clean" (Acts 10:15).

Right after he has this mysterious vision, Cornelius sends for him. The "unclean" Gentile asks to hear the good news of Jesus. Peter has no trouble making the connection. He understands that the vision was about the universality of God's love and commitment to every "nation."

The word *nation* is actually the Greek word *ethni* from which we derive our word *ethnic*. The term refers to a *race, culture,* or *people*. Peter makes the connection that, among every race, culture, or people, those who fear God and "do what is right" are eligible for baptism, for inclusion in the people of God.

This brings us back to the gay and lesbian tribal identity issue, only now we can see it in a biblical context. Is the gay and lesbian community just a political lobby for homosexual behavior, or are we an *ethni?* Certainly there are heterosexual people who engage in homosexual behavior, and gay and lesbian people who may never have sex at all. Are we a kind of behavior, or a kind of people for whom homoerotic attraction is one characteristic?

An *ethni* may be defined by a common history, vocabulary, dialect, culture, institutions (schools, libraries, clubs, churches, synagogues, social organizations, or businesses), heroes, political leaders, scholars, values, and the ability to recognize each other even when submerged in the dominant culture. If these constitute an *ethni,* gay and lesbian people are included in the word *nation* used in Acts 10:35.

What evidence of the gay and lesbian *ethni* exists in the Bible? This is a complex detective story made more difficult by thousands of years of heterosexist bias in secular history and biblical scholarship.

So let us begin at the beginning. I feel as though I need to give at least a nod to Adam and Eve. When fundamentalists realize that we have read the Bible and can intelligently refute their claims that the Bible condemns homosexuality, they often retreat to the most desperate argument, "What about Adam and Eve? Huh?"

OK, let's look at this story of the mother and father of us all, Adam and Eve. First of all, the first two chapters of Genesis give two distinct traditions about creation, both of which refer to the creation of humans. Much has been written on the theology and grammar of sexuality in those stories: most notably, Phyllis Trible's *God and the Rhetoric of Human Sexuality.*[45]

Scholars have long demonstrated the connections among various creation stories in the Ancient Near East. It is believed by some scholars that Israel borrowed and adapted traditions from surrounding cultures in the telling of both creation accounts in Genesis. Similarities to the creation stories of other indigenous peoples have also been analyzed. Justo Gonzales theorizes that "Genesis 1 and 2 [are] two different stories of creation placed side by side. They represent different tribal traditions."[46] In the past, these stories have been labeled by "author" (J and E), as if the differences were about individual authors' styles. Gonzales's observation makes more sense in a culture that values the tribal identity more than the individual's identity.

These, then, are not gay and lesbian tribal creation stories! If we are truly to *universalize* them, we must not see Adam and Eve as exclusive in their natures but inclusive. Another way to explore this is to ask the question, "Does the fact that God created gender differences automatically mean that sexuality must be monolithically heterosexual?" We do not make the claim that all of human life is simply a *clone* of Adam and Eve. God does seem to like variety as an aspect of creation: human beings are incredibly differentiated into racial, ethnic, size, shape, hue, and other physical and intellectual characteristics. Why would the fact that God created human beings as men and women mean that human beings were to have only one type of sexual identity? Why is it that we cannot see sexuality as a complex, interesting part of the variety of creation?

There is the argument about the "mechanics" of sex, as I call it. One churchwoman said to me, "But, see, look at human anatomy and what *fits* where!" This is the "penis-in-the-vagina" theory—the be-all and end-all of human sexual possibility.

I don't think it is our fault that some people lack sexual imagination. Frankly, lots of body parts can fit quite nicely in lots of places. And I'm sure it is wonderful that, for at least some heterosexuals, the *fit* of their penis and their vagina is quite pleasurable and that, as the Bible says, "It's good!" But there are endless ways—erotic, sensual, pleasurable—in which human beings can touch each other for their mutual health and enjoyment.

Let's face it; good old Adam and Eve have produced gay and lesbian children! And the fact that we are gay or lesbian does not negate our maleness or femaleness, despite what the annotators of 1 Corinthians 6:9 in the NRSV think! (See chapter 3.)

More threatening and perhaps also making this more complicated is John Money's theory that gender, like sexual orientation, is actually not dualistic but exists on a continuum! There are people who are toward the center of the continuum, and the rest of us are more or less male or female. The need for mythology and strong social sanctions to keep the gender differences "intact" is really understandable. If gender is more truly a *combination* of social construction, genetics, and physiology, then maybe the fundamentalists and patriarchs *do* have something to worry about. Maybe God didn't invent patriarchy, or rigid sex roles. Maybe those gender roles are not given, but change over time. Maybe the world never was monolithically heterosexual.

But let's get this "straight"—that isn't our fault. Adam and Eve, presumably Semites, had black, white, brown, fat, skinny, tall, short, smart, stupid, lovely, hateful, straight, bisexual, gay, and lesbian children. So don't blame us. Blame Adam and Eve—or, better yet, give God credit for our wonderful diversity!

One way to begin to get a handle on biblical views of a gay and lesbian anthropology is to try to understand biblical concepts of immortality.

The Hebrew Scriptures are not very clear about any consistent concept of life after death. The *Anchor Bible Dictionary* says:

> In the cosmology reflected throughout most of the Hebrew Bible, mortal humankind belongs on earth, not in heaven. At death, a person descends below to the netherworld known as Sheol. Psalm 115 expressed this succinctly:
>
> The heavens are the Lord's heavens,
> *but the earth he* [sic] *has given to human beings.*
> *The dead do not praise the Lord,*
> nor do any that go down into the silence.
> But we will bless the Lord from this time on and forever.
> Praise the Lord!

Generally speaking, just as there is no coming back from the dead, there is no idea or expectation that humans can go to heaven, a place reserved for God and his [sic] angelic attendants. This means that any report of a human being ascending to heaven would be seen as not only extraordinary, but often even as an intrusion or invasion of the divine realm.[47]

The concept that immortality might consist of "going to heaven" did begin to enter later Jewish thought and early Christianity, probably through Hellenistic influences. And contemporary American Jews and Christians often have similar ideas about heaven or the afterlife.

However, for most of the duration of biblical Judaism, the primary way one could achieve any sense of "immortality" was through one's descendants, one's children. Through them, you, your life, and your people lived on.

The cultural values of biblical-era Jews (and of Jews today) were more communal than those of Western Christians. The individual was not so important in himself or herself; he or she was important *insofar as he or she belonged to a people,* to a community. One way to express this belonging was through the bearing and raising of children.

The worst fate that could befall someone in such a culture and religion was to be *cut* off from one's people. There were three primary ways in which one could be cut off: by being exiled for certain crimes or afflictions, by public execution, or by dying without leaving any children. Those who were cut off were thought of as having been "cursed."

Conversely, prosperity and having many children were viewed as signs of God's favor and blessing (see, for example, Psalms 127:3–5 and 128:3–6). The entire story of Job is a wrestling with these very ancient concepts of curses and blessings, possessions and children as signs of God's favor.

In this context, female barrenness was considered to be the result of God's curse. A woman's self-worth and her worth in the society were directly connected to her ability to give her husband heirs. The immortality of both of them was at stake! The Bible is full of stories of women who desperately prayed to God to open their wombs. Sarah's inability to conceive children for Abraham led to her suggestion that Hagar become the first surrogate mother in the Bible. Rachel's grief over her initial childlessness and Hannah's prayer are also well-known examples. (See Psalms 113:9, Genesis 30:1, and 1 Samuel 10:1.) Luke opens his Gospel with the story of childless Zechariah and Elizabeth and how God blessed them with a son, John the Baptist, in their old age.

In addition, barrenness became a metaphor used by the prophets to describe Israel's pitiful condition when its people felt abandoned or cursed by God. Isaiah 54 begins with a powerful recasting of this metaphor:

> *Sing, O barren one who did not bear;*
> *burst into song and shout,*
> you *who have not been in labor!*
> For the children of the desolate woman will be more
> than the children of her that is married, says the Lord.
> Enlarge the site of your tent, and let the curtains of your habita-
> tions be stretched out; do not hold back; lengthen your cords
> *and strengthen* your *stakes. . . .*
> Do not fear, for you will not be ashamed;
> do not be discouraged, for you
> will not suffer disgrace;
> for you will forget the shame of your youth,
> and the disgrace for your widowhood you will remember no more.
> *Isaiah 54:1–2, 4*

Isaiah's prophetic message uses the metaphor of barrenness to represent Israel's condition: the "shame of [her] youth" represents pre-exile apostasy (faithlessness) and "widowhood" is a metaphor for the Exile. Women were "disgraced" by widowhood because it was considered an indicator that they had done something to put them in disfavor with God. It was financially and socially devastating to be widowed, and, even though it might have happened because of God's displeasure, Israel was also commanded to *care* for the widows and orphans in its midst (which, according to the prophets, they did better at some times than at others).

In this recasting of the metaphor, Israel is restored, and, like a barren, widowed woman with no hope of children, she is visited with God's favor and now becomes the mother of many children, even more than the children of "she who is married." She is vindicated.

Two chapters later, in Isaiah 56, Isaiah uses the term "dry tree" (in Hebrew, a feminine word that implied barrenness) in association with the word *eunuch* (verse 3). In verse 5 of Isaiah 56, the term "cut off" is used in association with the word *eunuch*. The way in which these terms and metaphors are mingled and associated (in nearby chapters and in the same verses), suggests that the term *eunuch* in Isaiah (and perhaps elsewhere, as we shall see) may really be a generic term used to refer to men and women who did not or could not produce children and were consequently "cursed" and "cut off."

The main reference in the Torah—the first five books of the Bible comprising core Jewish teaching—which required the exclusion of eunuchs from the Temple is Deuteronomy 23:1. It reads: "No one whose testicles are crushed or whose penis is cut off shall be admitted to the assembly of the Lord." Leviticus 21:17 says only those who are "unblemished can present themselves before God." This verse was apparently applied to eunuchs, who in some ancient pagan religions were temple priests.

But in the marvelous 56th chapter, Isaiah proclaims an inclusive covenant that promises that eunuchs and barren women, along with Gentiles, will someday have the right to full participation in the blessings of God and in the worshipping community. In this case, Isaiah stops speaking metaphorically and speaks quite literally to two groups of outcasts vis-à-vis temple worship:

> Do not let the foreigner joined to the Lord say,
> "The Lord will surely separate me from his [sic] people,"

and do not let the eunuch say, "I am just a dry tree."
For thus says the Lord:
"To the eunuchs who keep my Sabbaths,
who choose the things that please me
and hold fast my covenant,
I will give, in my house and within my walls,
a monument and a name better than sons and daughters;
I will give them an everlasting name
that shall not be cut off . . .
These I will bring to my holy mountain,
and make them joyful in my house of prayer;
their burnt offerings and their sacrifices will
be accepted on my altar;
for my house shall be called a house of prayer for all peoples."
Thus says the Lord God, who gathers the outcasts of Israel,
"I will gather others to them besides those already gathered."
Isaiah 56:4–5, 7–8

The word *accepted* that is found in the seventh verse has the very same root (using the Greek Septuagint version of the Hebrew Scriptures) as the Greek word *acceptable* in Acts 10:34–35. The context there is that story of Peter and Cornelius already discussed, in which Peter announces that "in every nation *[ethni, people]* anyone who fears God and does what is right is *acceptable* to God." So the connection of Isaiah 56 and Acts 10 is established in the word usage and theology.

Isaiah 56 is about the hope for future inclusion of those who were previously excluded from the worshipping community. Those who were outcasts and cut off because of their Gentile status or because of their sexuality will now be included. Eunuchs and barren women, I believe, *are our gay, lesbian, and bisexual antecedents.*[48] I also believe it is amazingly simple to demonstrate this. One very obvious point eluded me for a long time: it is in the actual words and structure of this section of Isaiah 56. In speaking about eunuchs, Isaiah says that God says, "I will make you a monument better than sons and daughters." If eunuchs were only males, or castrated males, then why would the words for both sons and daughters be used here? Eunuch is obviously a generic term for something!

In the typical style of the "politics of avoidance," the NRSV makes only this comment about the passage in Isaiah 56: "God himself [sic] will honor faithful eunuchs." This is a very tepid comment, to say the least, which gives no help in understanding the term *eunuch* or why Isaiah would be bothering to mention them in such a dramatic way. Isaiah is proposing changing very precious and sacred boundaries about the definition of Judaism.

The third edition of *The Annotated Oxford Bible* narrows the definition of eunuchs to the "sexually mutilated." It pairs eunuchs with foreigners who are converts as those who would be excluded from the temple by their status. Certainly castration is one definition of a eunuch, but the Bible suggests that the category of eunuch took on additional meaning and expands the ranks of those so labeled [page 1056, Hebrew Bible].

Who were the "eunuchs" of biblical times?

Until a few years ago, I would probably have said that the only eunuch I'd ever heard of in the Bible was the nameless Ethiopian eunuch baptized by Philip on the Gaza road in Acts 8. Most people aren't even aware of that story. I also assumed that the term *eunuch* had only one definition: a male who had been castrated.

But the Bible is virtually swarming with eunuchs! And there is *more than one* definition or understanding of what the term *eunuch* actually means.

Under "Eunuch," the *Anchor Bible Dictionary* says, "*Eunuch.* See Palestine, Administration of Post-exilic Judean Officials" and "*Eunuch, Ethiopian.* See Ethiopian Eunuch."[49]

Let's begin with "Palestine, Administration of." As technical as this passage is, I think it is very crucial in making my argument:

> 4. *saris* - Eunuch. Its Akkadian origin is *sa-resi*, "he who is chief." In 1 Kings 22:9 the saris is exactly the kind of official for minor errands which concerns us here. But he is usually a much higher and foreign official; as in Genesis 37–38; Esther 1:10–11; and 2 Kings 18:17. Though such an official was often called "eunuch" in the Orient, BDB [Brown-Driver Briggs lexicon of the Bible] is rather outdated in assigning this as its principal meaning and relating it to admittedly demonstrative verbs for castrate in Syriac, Aramaic, and Arabic. Hence, it will prove relevant to the long-standing debate as to whether Nehemiah (la) was really a eunuch, as in the corresponding Greek (2 Esdras 11:11). ... Even if Nehemiah was called "eunuch," this term, like

our "chamberlain," may have really signified some administrative office. If so, it would seem to have been of a higher and more privileged rank than the local officials being discussed here.[50]

I have a theory about the role of eunuchs, especially in the Hebrew Bible: that eunuchs often appear on the scenes as *messengers* and *go-betweens* and are often involved in palace intrigue in the Jewish or foreign royal courts.

This theory or observation, perhaps more than any other, correlates to Judy Grahn's and Mark Thompson's theories of gay and lesbian tribal identities. If gay men, particularly, were *berdache* (spiritual go-betweens, mediators between earthly parties and between heaven and earth), shamans, and magicians in ancient cultures, why wouldn't they also show up in that role in the Bible? They certainly do. And in the Bible these people are called eunuchs. The eunuchs in the Joseph story and the Esther story are notable in this regard. And this is certainly the role of Nehemiah, which the NRSV says was as "a palace servant of Artaxerxes I at Susa in Elam,"[51] the winter residence of the Persian kings. The word *eunuch (saris)* appears 17 times in the Hebrew Bible, and there are other references to persons in similar roles. Furthermore, the *eunuchs serve a subversive role in the palaces of Israel's enemies.* They act as a kind of palace double agent; they are spies and sources of information (palace gossips). This reminds me of the old insider gay aphorism: "Telegraph, telephone, tell-a-queen!"

In some cases, these eunuchs actually go against their own bosses (and kings) and rescue the prophets, kings, queens, or spokespersons of God. One really important example of this is the Ethiopian eunuch in Jeremiah 38:7–13. At the risk of his own life, Ebed-melech, the Ethiopian, "a eunuch in the king's house," rescues Jeremiah by pulling him out of a cistern. Jeremiah, the unmarried prophet, was being held there, waiting to be murdered by his own people. Ebed-melech becomes the agent of God in rescuing Jeremiah. Interestingly, the NRSV has this to say about Ebed-melech: "Ironically, Jeremiah was delivered from murder . . . by a court official (who was not necessarily a eunuch physically)."[52] The more recent third edition is virtually the same [page 1139, Hebrew Bible].

So, if he was not *necessarily a eunuch physically,* in what sense was he a eunuch? How does the NRSV know of more than one kind of eunuch? And why the association of eunuchs with castrati? One documented fact is that there were boys who were raised to become court servants or officials, and they were castrated so they could safely administer the palace household and be trusted not to impregnate the queen or princesses. They were castrated in order to preserve social order, to safeguard caste and class, through preserving the royal bloodline. Such castrati sometimes would still have heterosexual sex without ejaculating sperm, although many became functionally homosexual. It may also be that young men who were noticed to be gay were also groomed for these positions because it would be obvious that they would not be interested in impregnating the queen or princesses. If many ancient cultures managed to acknowledge the special gifts of gay and lesbian people, why not the cultures of the ancient peoples who are referred to in the Bible?

So, the term *eunuch* may have referred to a role that was *stereotyped* as one meant for castrati, gay men, or the occasional safe, highly efficient, trustable straight man. There are, as we know, occasional heterosexual male interior decorators and hairdressers—they're just not very common! In fact, the modern association of castrati with gay men may simply be a homophobic one—that is, all gay men are socially "emasculated," in modern cultures in particular.

Once we expand the definition of *eunuchs,* they of course become potentially a larger group of people. Isaiah, in chapter 56, chose two groups of people to symbolize the future expansion of the "people of God," thereby including those who had previously been excluded: eunuchs and Gentiles. If eunuchs were only castrated males, that would seem to be an awfully small group of people to prophesy about. Also, the NRSV annotators obviously agree that some eunuchs were "not eunuchs physically." It would be interesting to know why they think this particular *saris* in Jeremiah was not a castrati kind of eunuch (do they think he was also not gay?). Is it because they think that a castrati wouldn't be that important an official? Or wouldn't he have been *butch* enough to be able to get Jeremiah out of the cistern? And it is clear in any case that whatever the sexual orientation of eunuchs, Isaiah viewed them as people who are *barren,* who do not reproduce, and who are therefore *cut off.*

The stories of Ebed-melech and of other faithful eunuchs before him make Isaiah's prophecy easier to understand. God wants to honor eunuchs, foreign and domestic, who have themselves already been faithful to God! God is overturning the restrictions on admission to "the people of God" based on physical characteristics, sexual status, or ability to reproduce.

I will demonstrate that this prophecy is actually fulfilled in the New Testament, as is the prophecy of the inclusion of the Gentiles. But I have never seen anywhere, except in writings by gay or lesbian theologians, even the barest research on the connections among the various references and prophecies about eunuchs in the Bible.

One of the most startling references to eunuchs in the New Testament was made by Jesus. He speaks about eunuchs in a passage that is one of the most *under-commented* on in all of the Gospels: Matthew 19:10–12. These verses occur in the context of a discussion about divorce. Jesus is taking a hard line about divorce, and the disciples complain, saying, "Well, if you're going to be that strict about divorce, maybe it's better not to marry!" To which Jesus replies that this injunction against heterosexual divorce does *not* apply to everyone:

> For there are eunuchs who have been so by birth, and there are eunuchs who have been made eunuchs by others, and there are eunuchs who have made themselves eunuchs *for the sake of the kingdom of heaven.* Let anyone accept this who can.

It is amazing to me that neither the story of Philip and the Ethiopian eunuch, nor the story of Ebed-melech in Jeremiah, nor Isaiah's prophecy in Isaiah 56 are cross-referenced in the NRSV with Matthew 19—or in *any* Bible or standard commentary! These are the politics of biblical interpretation at their most subtle and at their worst. Such gross omission and silence obscure the possible relationship of these passages.

Furthermore, I have never seen any commentary on Matthew 19 that acknowledges that Jesus spoke of a *typology* of eunuchs. Obviously, Jesus knew that there was *more than one way* to become labeled as a eunuch. The annotation in the NRSV states simply, "Jesus recognizes a place for voluntary celibacy in the service of God's kingdom." Voluntary celibacy? That's all? What about the other two categories? Do the annotators think they are self-explanatory? Okay, suppose we agree that "making themselves eunuchs for the sake of the kingdom of God" is about voluntary celibacy and that, perhaps, "being made eunuchs by others" covers the castrati, but who are *"eunuchs from birth"*?

If "eunuchs from birth" are intersex or those with birth defects that affect the male genitals, just how many people are we talking about here? Statistically, children who are intersex are born in less than one in

100,000 births. It is unlikely that Jesus met more than 10,000 people in his lifetime—and even that estimate would be pushing it. The likelihood of him coming across such a person is remote. So, who are the "eunuchs from birth"? Are they those to whom the rules about heterosexual marriage may not apply? I have a clue, and I think John McNeill, in his book *The Church and the Homosexual,* was the first to say it: gay and lesbian people!

We used to see a pamphlet—produced, I think, by Evangelicals Concerned (a gay and gay-friendly evangelical group started by Dr. Ralph Blair) —that said on the cover, "What Jesus Said about Homosexuality." You would turn to the inside, and there was a blank page! On the back page, it said, "That's right, he said absolutely nothing." We thought that was cute and comforting. Thank God, at least Jesus kept his mouth shut about us. Big sigh of relief.

But I think it's not true. I think Jesus spoke about us and to us in Matthew 19. What this passage says to me is "Let anyone accept this who can": It's as if he calls out, "Yoo-hoo! Homosexuals, listen up! This one's for you!" So he did speak about us, to us, and said, "I know who you are, and you are included, too."

But the real capstone in this chain of prophecy and fulfillment lies in the story of Philip and the Ethiopian eunuch (Acts 8:26–40).

What is fascinating about this story in Acts is that it is the story of yet another Ethiopian eunuch, and I find no commentary anywhere that acknowledges that there are two Ethiopian eunuchs in the Bible. Bible commentators who spend paragraphs on obscure and remote associations *never* link these two characters. I call it *eunuch phobia.* For that matter, the racism of the white-dominated biblical "scholar guild" could mean it is also *Ethiopian phobia.*

There are contrasting views of cultural "stereotypes" of Ethiopian eunuchs: Herbert Lockyer states that Ebed-melech was "a credit to his class" (not race, but *class*!).[53] Lockyer seems to have information that eunuchs were considered a *class* or *caste* of person. In addition, he states, as a generalization: "The Eastern Eunuchs were a *pitiless, cruel race,* whose delight was to wound and vex."[54] Well, that sounds like some drag queens I've come across! "Priscilla [Ebed-melech] Queen of the Desert" eunuchs were a *bitchy* class? He also called him "the benevolent eunuch" in a way that sounds an awful lot like the "Good Samaritan," meant to be an oxymoron.

Beverly Roberts Gavents also writes about the Ethiopian eunuch of Acts 8 in the *Anchor Bible Dictionary*. She says:

> What has puzzled interpreters is that Luke identifies this particular Ethiopian as a eunuch, which means that he *cannot have been a proselyte to Judaism* (cf. Deut 23:1 and Joseph Ant. 4:290–91), despite the fact that he has been to Jerusalem to worship and is reading from a scroll of Isaiah as he travels (8:27–38). . . . Interestingly, Luke himself does not comment on the restrictions about converting eunuchs, which may suggest that Luke is less interested in that feature of the story than he is in some others. For example, eunuchs frequently held places of respect and trust in Eastern courts, as does this one, and the identification of this figure as a eunuch may simply reinforce the reader's impression that he is an *unusual person*. . . . Within the story, the Ethiopian's actions underscore this portrayal of him as an intriguing, romantic, even exotic personage.

The Ethiopian, coming as he does *from the end of the earth,* stands at the threshold of the worldwide mission. He prefigures Cornelius. Small wonder the early church writers pass along a tradition that the Ethiopian [eunuch] returned to his own country and preached a gospel message there.[55]

This author thinks that the Ethiopian's "eunuch-ness" is just incidental and just serves to make him more exotic. This is a profound trivialization of the meaning of this story.

Gavents does not pick up that in the story the eunuch is reading the *Book of Isaiah*. He in fact is reading from Isaiah 53:7–8 (awfully close to Isaiah 54 and 56!), which among other things details the fate and destiny of the Suffering Servant, whom Christians identify with Jesus, the Messiah. In that description (53:8), Isaiah states:

> By a perversion of justice he was taken away.
> Who could have imagined his future?
> For he was cut off from the land of the living,
> stricken for the transgression of my people.

It is not *incidental* that Luke quotes this passage of Isaiah or that the eunuch wanted to understand it. The term "cut off" is a reference to the curse that was placed on anyone who was *exiled, executed by capital punishment,* or *did not reproduce.* The Ethiopian eunuch was reading a prophecy of a Messiah *with whom he could identify!* The Messiah was someone who, like him, was cut off, not able to be a part, not able to enjoy the gift of immortality.

The eunuch had reason to believe that there was hope that those who had been cut off—who had not previously been eligible—would now be eligible. When he asked Philip what was to prevent him from being baptized (he was ineligible before on *two* counts: being Gentile and being a eunuch), Philip is silent in the text and simply baptizes him. And we don't even know his name. The nameless eunuch, the patron saint of Ethiopian Christians, a black gay man, becomes the first African Christian, and the most clear and complete fulfillment of the prophecy of Isaiah 56, that God's house would become a "house of prayer for all people."

6 • Jesus Was a Eunuch—And a Lover

Jesus often said, "Whoever has ears, let them hear," because people can read the scriptures over and over and not comprehend or follow their guidance. Let us bring open eyes, ears, and hearts to the joyful task of finding ourselves in the Bible.

My favorite eunuchs of the Bible are in the wonderful story of the magi in Matthew's narrative of Jesus' infancy. It is a tale of eunuchs. It doesn't say there were *three* wise ones; post-biblical legend invented that number. Matthew's second chapter is devoted to these mysterious foreign strangers who visit the infant (or toddler) Jesus.

Our Christmas crèches always combine the Luke and Matthew infancy narratives, which are almost mutually exclusive in their content. We just put everyone (shepherds, angels, wise men) there together at the manger at the same time.

Matthew 2 tells a story of what *The New Oxford Annotated Bible* calls "three wise men, a learned class in ancient Persia."[56] They were Zoroastrian priests, astrologers, magicians, ancient shamans from the *courts* of ancient Persia. They were the equivalent of Merlin of Britain. They were sorcerers, high-ranking officials, but not kings—definitely not kings. But, quite possibly, they were *queens*. We've always pictured them with elaborate, exotic, unusual clothing—quite festive, highly decorated and accessorized! But, not until I recognized that they were probably eunuchs did I realize that never *once* did I imagine that their wives accompanied them on this trip! Deep down, I never thought of them as having wives.

Also, the wise eunuchs, shamans, holy men were the only ones who had the forethought to go shopping before they visited the baby Jesus! This seems to me to be an obvious gay clue!

They also have shamanistic dreams. They deceive evil King Herod and actually play the *precise* role that many other prominent eunuchs play in the Bible: they rescue the prophet, this time the Messiah of God, and foil the evil royal plot against God's anointed. It's a classic gay/eunuch drama!

I mean, who were those guys? They get a whole chapter in Matthew and then disappear forever from the scene (another classic eunuch trait). They are foreigners. They are pagans. They are "queer"! They are heroes, and their images grace millions of homes, windows, churchyards, chancels, children's pageants, musicals, and hymns every Advent and Christmas. Just think of all those children in their father's bathrobes in Christmas pageants every year, trying to portray three queens in semi-drag! Jesus had gay *fairy godmothers* who dropped in on him and saved his life, so he could save ours. What a great book! What a Savior!

From his auspicious birth, Jesus became the fulfillment of the Suffering-Servant prophecy of Isaiah 53. He was "cut off" from his people in two ways: he was executed as a criminal, and he presumably died without heirs. What the Ethiopian eunuch and the early scribe of the book of Acts suggest was that there was a connection between the Eunuch, Isaiah, and Jesus. The obvious connection that scholars have refused to hear is that Jesus was a functional, if not physical, eunuch (like Ebed-melech?). The life, death, and resurrection of Jesus Christ, furthermore, redefined for the new emerging Christian community the way in which one achieves eternal life. No longer was eternal life achieved through bearing children but through one's identification with the risen Christ.

The whole "family" and "family values" issue is critical in looking at the issue of gays and lesbians in the Bible. The belief that there is an "ideal" or "normal" family and that everyone who doesn't "fit" that family model is somehow lacking is a politically motivated sham.

As we pointed out earlier, when confronted by his biological family (mother, brothers, and sisters), Jesus pointed to his disciples as his new family and said, "For whoever does the will of God is my brother and sister and mother" (Mark 3:31).

The Bible, in fact, knows almost nothing of the post-Reformation ideal of monogamous, lifelong, romantic heterosexual marriage. Heterosexual marriages, in fact, were not performed inside Christian churches until the second millennium. The Bible includes examples of marriage relationships that are based on political and property considerations; ones that are the product of international politics, that are essentially business transactions; as well as polygamy, extended families, Levirate marriages (in which a man was obligated to marry his brother's widow), and other lifestyles. The anti-marriage bias in the New Testament and the negative emphasis on sex of early Christian theologians (we can probably blame this on the Hellenists, too!) are well documented by experts in human sexuality.

Virginia Mollenkott has a wonderful appendix to her book *Sensuous Spirituality* that lists 18 "diverse forms of family mentioned or implied in the Hebrew and Christian Scriptures." The appendix then goes on to include 22 "additional forms of family mentioned or implied in the Hebrew and Christian Scriptures suggested by participants at Families 2000"—a conference *sponsored by the National Council of Churches of Christ* (Chicago, April 1991).[57]

The myth—actually the lie—that said *the* approved form of biblical family consists of a romantic, lifelong monogamous heterosexual couple (with 2.3 kids) is amazing in its persistence and its powerful influence. Only something like 11 percent of families in the United States live in such a configuration. The way the rest of us live—in what are called "alternative families" (even though they are alternatives to a small minority lifestyle)—is actually much more like the varied family configurations of the Bible!

The so-called nuclear family is an invention of post-Reformation, industrial Western society. Yet, at least in the United States, people who pontificate about family values and who put down the rest of us have been able to bully the politicians, the leaders of our country, and have misused the Bible to do it.

One way to get at this is to ask the question, where in the Bible do you find a clear, incontrovertible example of that "nuclear family"? Every family in the Bible seems to have its *unusual* aspects or complications. The only heterosexual *couples* explicitly mentioned in the whole New Testament that I am aware of are Joseph and Mary (not by any means an *ordinary* relationship); Zachariah and Elizabeth—saved from being "cut off" by a late-life pregnancy; Peter and his wife, but only by inference (because Jesus heals Peter's mother-in-law, we assume he was married or widowed); Priscilla and Aquilla (if, that is, *Aquilla* is truly a male name); and Ananias and Sapphira, who died suddenly in Acts. There are no other heterosexual couples actually identified in the entire New Testament. Paul does complain at one point that some apostles get to bring their wives along on missionary trips, and this indicates that some of them were married (1 Corinthians 9:5).

I always thought it was interesting that Paul feels the necessity to say, in 1 Timothy 3:12, "Let deacons be the husband of one wife." In the NRSV they translate it differently for the first time (although they acknowledge the literal wording, they give no explanation for their revised translation). It now reads, "Let deacons be married only *once*." In any case, the fact that Paul has to say this meant that Christians either *did* marry more than once (enough so that Paul would have to make special mention of this restriction for deacons only) or that the people who were being evangelized in the Hellenistic world (outside of Palestine) were still practicing forms of polygamy, which the church had not entirely outlawed. Why else would Paul feel compelled to mention it?

This is just one example of the ways in which we need to read *between the lines* and ask questions about the inferences about marriage in the Hebrew and Christian Scriptures.

What Kind of Family Did Jesus Have?

There have been some books that speculate about Jesus' marriage and family, but not very many.[58] Most people's superficial view of Jesus' family life is that Jesus grew up in a small town with his mother and father and (if you're not Catholic) with brothers and sisters; that Jesus' father probably died before his public ministry began (although this is never stated, it is a widely held assumption). The prevailing assumption is also that Jesus was celibate all his adult life—he never married—and he considered his mother and Nazareth his home base.

Besides Nazareth, there are two other places that are referred to in the Gospels as Jesus' home: Capernaum (Mark 2:1) and the home of Mary, Martha, and Lazarus in Bethany.

In a different way, the Temple in Jerusalem is also home for Jesus. In the only story of Jesus' childhood in the canonical Scriptures, Jesus gets separated from his biological family as they are returning from Jerusalem to Nazareth. They go back to Jerusalem to look for him and finally discover him, after three days (an interesting parallel to the resurrection), talking to the teachers in the Temple. Jesus is in his *Abba's* house

(Aramaic for "Father" or "Daddy," and some even say "Mommy") and feels at home there. The story records his mother upbraiding him for worrying them and "treating us like this." Is Jesus apologetic? Sorry for worrying and alarming them like that? No. His answer is actually quite surly (or perhaps even *snotty*): "Why were you searching for me? Did you not know I must be in my Father's house?" (Luke 2:49).

Jesus, at age 12 (a typical preteen in some ways), thinks his parents *just don't get it*. In fact, the Bible *says* they didn't understand him (the battle cry of adolescence!).

But this may also be a clue that Jesus' familial relationships were already a little strained—not "ordinary." In my lighter moments, I imagine this as every parent's nightmare: not only is your adolescent a know-it-all and doesn't want to be seen with you in public, but, on top of that, your kid really *is* God (or the Messiah)!

One of the areas that intrigues me is the relationship of Jesus to his father, Joseph. On one hand, only Matthew includes anything about Joseph. Matthew portrays Joseph as the faithful Jew, obedient to God's demands, and a protective agent of the Messiah (a little bit like the role of a eunuch). On the other hand, although Luke includes both Mary and Joseph in the story of Jesus' boyhood, only Mary speaks.

The assumption that Joseph has died by the time Jesus begins his ministry is an interesting one. If Joseph was in his twenties or thirties or older when Jesus was born, his dying is very plausible. One also wonders if Jesus waited to begin his ministry until after his father died, and if so, why? What was their relationship like? Was Joseph still alive during part or all of Jesus' ministry? Was he disapproving? Joseph just *disappears* in the New Testament—vanishes without a trace like so many fathers (and like a lot of the eunuchs). Jesus fits the old psychoanalytical (and erroneous!) profile of a homosexual man: an absent father and an overprotective, domineering mother!

Why is it that scholars have never pursued the subject of Jesus' relationship with Joseph? What kinds of issues might this raise that would be difficult or challenging to our traditional views of Jesus' family life? This is especially compelling, because it is still taboo in orthodox circles to see Joseph as Jesus' biological father.

Gay men and lesbians can easily understand Jesus' problems with his family's lack of understanding of his identity as the Messiah. Gays and lesbians, unlike racial and ethnic minorities, often find themselves feeling and being different from their family members. Not sharing your identity or minority status with most or all of your family members is very isolating and alienating.

In "coming out" as the Messiah, Jesus experienced alienation from his biological family, at least at first. We lesbians and gay men understand this very well.

So, Jesus had four homes: with his biological family in Nazareth, in Capernaum (we're not sure why); in the Temple (God's house is his home); and with Mary, Martha, and Lazarus. In another sense, however, Jesus is *homeless*. He is at home nowhere: "Foxes have holes, and birds of the air have nests, but the Son of humanity has nowhere to lay his head" (Luke 9:58). Jesus began his life *away* from his home in Nazareth, unable to find "room at the inn" in Bethlehem. There is a tension between Jesus being at home in lots of places (no one home or family structure could contain him, could be adequate for him, could completely claim or own him) and his never quite being at home anywhere.

We get a little view of family life for Jesus in John 2. Jesus' mother attends a wedding in Cana, nine miles northwest of Galilee. There is no mention of his father. (Dad hated weddings? Was he dead, or ill, or a workaholic?) This could have been the wedding of a cousin or other relative or of relatives of friends from Nazareth. Jesus *and the disciples* are invited. I wonder if those who are giving the wedding feast invited only Jesus, but he asked if the disciples could come. Or they invited Mary and Jesus, and she told them, "Oh, he'll only come if he can bring the whole gang!" Part of the style of Jesus' ministry and life was that these disciples were now a part of his extended family and social life as well. John 2:12 amplifies and corroborates this "blended-family" reality of Jesus' life:

> After this [the wedding in Cana] he [Jesus] went down to Capernaum with his mother, his brother, and his disciples; and they remained there a few days.

Capernaum is on the northern shore of the Sea of Galilee, so they were having a few days *at the shore*. Maybe they decided to do a little fishing, resting, and strategizing. At this stage, the family and disciples are still somewhat blended, in contrast to later stories (like the one in Mark

3:31) in which Jesus' biological family seems to have been *replaced* by this *family of disciples.*

But even as we try to understand the disciples as Jesus' primary community or family, there are myths and assumptions to overcome. Jesus did call 12 male disciples to be the core of this new community. However, in many places in the Gospel the term *disciples* has a broader meaning that includes all those who followed Jesus—those in the crowds and the "camp followers." Many scholars believe that the limiting identification of the "twelve disciples" was written back into the Gospels. One passage from Luke 8 (verses 1–3) adds some very important information to this picture of who was providing support for the blended family or movement of disciples:

> Soon afterward he went on through cities and villages, proclaiming and bringing the good news of the Kingdom of God. The twelve were with him, as well as some women who had been cured of evil spirits and infirmities: Mary, called Magdalene, from whom seven demons had gone out, and Joanna, the wife of Herod's steward Chuza, and Susanna, and many others who provided for them [other authorities say "him"] out of their resources.

Now, let's see if we understand this! Jesus was traveling around the countryside (staying in homes, camping out?) with 12 men, one of whom had a mother-in-law and presumably a wife; but, in addition, women traveled with them. One of these women had been healed of what would today probably be labeled a severe psychosis and was probably still recovering from years of social ostracism, pain, and rejection. Then there was Joanna, the wife of a man whose job is called "domestic administrator" (a court official, a eunuch?), and *many* others (women) who supported them (or "him," meaning Jesus) financially. Well, no wonder his family began to wonder if he was crazy; no wonder they came to get him! In a society that strictly regulated social contact between women and men, this was more than highly irregular. He travelled with married women without their husbands, who were there because Jesus had healed them. Probably some of them were *in love* with him, deep into what psychologists would call "transference," grateful to have been helped by a gentle man who actually noticed them and cared that they were suffering. There were also, single, abused, and abandoned women, recovering from mental, spiritual, and physical illnesses. Probably many of the men were following him for the same reason—all of them wanting Jesus' attention, wanting to be a part of the new community.

The fact that Jesus accepted the money or other kinds of support from these women is also amazing in his cultural context. Imagine the scorn he and both the male and female disciples had to put up with for that alone! And *all* the men were benefiting from the support of these women. Imagine what names they were called.

What do we think Chuza, Herod's "domestic administrator" thought or said when his wife came to him and said, "See you later, honey; I'm emptying our bank account and going off with some women friends to follow Jesus and his disciples. Be back in a few weeks, maybe." Do you think he said, "Have a wonderful time; you're in my prayers. I think I'll ask Herod for a donation"? I doubt it. What did other family members think? What were the consequences of the fact that Jesus and his followers broke many societal rules to do this ministry?

And just what was life really like on the road? Even if the understanding was that the members of this new family group were to be sexually faithful to whatever husbands or wives were back home (who may or may not have been filing for divorce!) or committed to an ideal of celibacy if they were single—the social, emotional, and sexual dynamics, the attractions and jealousies must have been incredible to try to manage. And think of the sleeping arrangements and the day-to-day issues of being part of an eclectic, co-sexual nomadic community that did not have any of the same structures that these folks had been used to all their lives. It is unrealistic and naive not to consider these issues. Also, there must have been tremendous excitement, urgency, and gratitude for the kind of loving fellowship that we only get glimpses of. All these people were there because they had been *touched by Jesus* and invited to go along. We read of others whom Jesus heals who ask to be allowed to come along, but Jesus tells them to go home instead. Was this sometimes because the traveling road show was getting complicated—too complicated to include more people?

Jesus also had a way of engaging complete strangers in an immediate, intimate way. The Gospels talk frequently about him feeling love and compassion for strangers, seeing into their hearts, feeling sorry for the lost and lonely crowds.

Were there children in his community? We certainly do read of the children who come to be blessed and the male disciples who want to shoo them away. But were there eventually children who actually traveled with Jesus' new community? If there were "many women," as it says in Luke 8, then I have to think there must have been some children traveling with them. It's hard to believe that they would have all been willing or able to leave the children behind. What was it like for these children? Or for the children whose mothers or fathers did leave them behind to be cared for by single parents or other family members?

Clearly, there are many unresolved issues about Jesus' home and family life. How much have traditional theologies read their own cultural mores and biases and lifestyles back into New Testament times? Certainly, I will be accused of doing that! However, all biblical commentators and certainly most preachers do that frequently. Dr. Thomas Hanks, a Presbyterian missionary in Argentina who is also a member of Metropolitan Community Church, has this to say in the *Anchor Bible Dictionary* about these biases:

> Liberation theologians have scarcely even raised any question about New Testament perspectives on despised sexual minorities and uncleanness (Countryman, 1988). Medieval monks assumed the New Testament to represent the perspective of continent bachelors; Protestantism has tended to assume that everyone except Paul must have had a wife and children. The failure to challenge sexual and family ideological assumptions has been a glaring weakness in theological efforts to delineate New Testament perspectives on oppression and poverty (Greenberg, 1988).[59]

It is very important, in a lesbian hermeneutic of the Bible, to "challenge sexual and family assumptions," especially about Jesus. The dominant assumption about Jesus has been that he was monolithically heterosexual or even asexual. For too long Jesus, and other New Testament characters, in particular, have been portrayed by the church as biblical versions of "genitalia-free" Barbie and Ken dolls. For Jesus to be accessible to new generations, in a new millennium, we will need to have the courage to read the same texts with new eyes, without those limiting assumptions. We must be willing to see ourselves in Jesus' experiences and choices about family and relationship.

We turn now to what J. D. Hastings, in an older commentary entitled *The Greater Men and Women of the Bible*, called "That most interesting of all New Testament households, the Bethany family."[60] Hastings also calls Bethany Jesus' "home away from home."[61] Bethany was less than two miles from Jerusalem. There is some dispute among Bible scholars about whether or not there are two towns called Bethany. In any case, Jesus is said to have been baptized at the Jordan River near Bethany, and he actually ascended into heaven just outside of Bethany. In the Synoptics (the Gospels of Matthew, Mark, and Luke), Jesus made Bethany his headquarters during his final week (Mark 11:11–12; Matt. 21:17; Luke 19:74). Jesus was anointed there, either by a nameless woman at Simon the leper's home or by Mary at the home of Mary, Martha, and Lazarus. Bethany was the last station for pilgrims on their way from Jordan to Jerusalem. And, in John 12, it is the launching place from which the crowd marches into Jerusalem on Palm Sunday.

I have sometimes wondered if we might someday find a long-lost "Bethany gospel" that might solve some of the mysteries of the Bethany community and of Jesus' relationship to Mary, Martha, and Lazarus, his adult family of choice. Perhaps John's Gospel really is (in part) a Bethany Gospel.

On the one hand, Mary, Martha, and Lazarus are the *only persons mentioned by name* whom Jesus *loved*. The others are the *beloved disciples* (more about that later) and the nameless rich young ruler who turns away from Jesus' invitation to follow him.

John McKenzie, in the *Dictionary of the Bible*, says that there is an "old unsolved problem" about Mary, Martha, and Lazarus that seems to relate to differences in the Synoptic and Johannine traditions.[62] John's Gospel treats the story of the raising of Lazarus from the dead (John 11) as the pinnacle of Jesus' ministry. It is his most impressive miracle, on the one hand, and it seals his fate, on the other. It is the longest account of any miracle, and it contains a great deal of detail, dialogue, and symbolism, in typical Johannine fashion. Also, after the resurrection of Lazarus, crowds begin to form in Bethany to see Lazarus and Jesus, and the Pharisees begin to seek Lazarus's life as well as that of Jesus (John 12:10). Jesus and Lazarus become paired as dangerous threats to the religious establishment. It is that post-resurrection-of-Lazarus *Bethany crowd* that marches into Jerusalem on Palm Sunday.

In contrast, the Synoptic Gospels (Matthew, Mark, and Luke) *do not even mention Lazarus*. Luke has Jesus tell a parable, "The Rich Man and Lazarus" (Luke 16), that is about a poor fictional character. Most scholars believe this character is totally unrelated to the brother of Mary and Martha.

Even more curiously, Luke does in fact mention Mary and Martha in the famous story in Luke 10:38. He oddly omits any mention of Lazarus. In this account, Bethany is not mentioned, just "a certain village," and Martha is named as the householder. Why the mysterious reference to location? In John 11, Mary and Martha are well-known persons who live in Bethany. *Who's Who in the Bible* comments, "It is strange that there is no further mention of Lazarus and his family in the history of the early Christian church at Jerusalem."[63]

The story of the raising of Lazarus is corroborated by one non-canonical source, the Secret Gospel of Mark, a Gnostic Gospel. Eastern Orthodox tradition says he was shipwrecked and became the bishop of Kitionum on Cyprus. Western Christian sources say he became first bishop of Marseilles and that Mary and Martha became missionaries to France.

Some scholars theorize that the sources of the Synoptic Gospels represent a kind of cumulative "anti-Lazarus" feeling, brought about by the idea that his resurrection caused the hastening of Jesus' death. Other scholars theorize that John exaggerated this story, that it is not as reliable as other miracle stories in the Gospels, and that it is meant to be a symbolic story, with Lazarus as the representation of all Christians who will die and be raised with Christ.

One very fascinating aspect of all this is the connection to the mystery of the "beloved disciple."

I found Vernard Eller's book, *The Name of the Beloved Disciple*, published in 1987, to be totally credible, and it convinced me that Lazarus *was* the beloved disciple.[64] Tradition favors the view that John (son of Zebedee) was the beloved disciple. In fact, the identity of the beloved disciple is never overtly stated; it is only implied. There is a connection to the probably pseudonymous author of the Book of John.

Eller's arguments are very well made. He gives ample evidence for the *unlikeliness* of John as the beloved disciple and makes a good case for Lazarus. Eller hypothesizes that Lazarus, like Nicodemus and Joseph of Arimathea, was a member of the Jewish intelligentsia and therefore a great threat, as Jesus' disciple, to the religious establishment. Consider these points:

- The term "beloved disciple" is *only* used in the Gospel of John (which was not actually written by the disciple John), and the term only appears *after* the resurrection of Lazarus. It first occurs in the description of the Last Supper, where the beloved disciple *lies on the breast of Jesus*. A very poignant scene, if this is the newly raised Lazarus. Eller points out that this would increase the jealousy of the twelve disciples toward Lazarus. Also, in the story of the raising of Lazarus, Lazarus is referred to as "he whom you [Jesus] love" (John 11:3).

- Eller develops an elaborate schematic diagram that shows how the fourth Gospel has carefully paired a Mary (Mary-L) with Lazarus in certain episodes and thereafter pairs a Mary (Mary Magdalene) with the beloved disciple in other episodes.

- Eller connects Lazarus and the one labeled "another disciple" to the disciple who had influence with the family of the high priest during Jesus' trial (John 18:12–27).

- Eller proposes that Lazarus and Mary *Magdalene* were offering Jesus' mother a new home in Bethany after Jesus' death and resurrection (John 19:23–37).

- Eller has a theory about Galilean disciples and Judean disciples being in ethnic regional competition and often being paired for balance. This would fit if Peter and the beloved disciple (Lazarus, not John) rushed to the empty tomb together (John 20:1–18). Eller's contention is *not* that Lazarus is a plausible guess but that Lazarus is the *best* guess among all the possibilities to be the beloved disciple.[65]

This brings up some other issues for us, then, in understanding the story of Jesus, Mary, Martha, and Lazarus.

First of all, only Mary and Martha speak: Lazarus never says a word, even as the beloved disciple. From an older commentary by Alexander White, we read:

Lazarus's ... name is never to be read in the New Testament till the appointed time comes when he is to be sick ... to die, and to be raised from the dead for the glory of God. *Nor is his voice heard. Lazarus loved silence, he sought obscurity. He liked to be overlooked. He reveled in neglect... The very Evangelists pass over Lazarus as if he were a worm and no man.*[66]

Obviously, Whyte's writing is archaic, but he does make some interesting observations about Lazarus and his silence. It is as if Lazarus is almost in some kind of a closet, isn't it?

Years ago, West Hollywood Presbyterian Church, inspired by Chris Glaser, founded the Lazarus Project, an outreach to gay men and lesbians. They used the name Lazarus because they compared the experience of being in the *tomb* to the experience of being closeted. Also, when Jesus raised Lazarus, he used the words "Come out" (John 11:43)!

However, it is quite another thing even to begin to suggest or think that Lazarus might have been homosexual. Perhaps he loved Jesus, had a crush on Jesus. We don't really know how old Lazarus was. Did he and Jesus have a platonic but distinctly homosexual relationship? How did he die the first time? The second? Was he the victim of a gay bashing? Did the authors of the Synoptic Gospels want to disguise and cover this up? Was the Gospel of John more free of "homo-hatred"? Were suspicions of "homoerotic" particular friendships and unusual "family" arrangements part of the reason people were attracted to the Jesus movement—and part of some other people's desire to persecute them?

Was Lazarus silenced for Jesus' protection or for the protection of the early Christian church leaders and authorities? Was he silenced "for his own good"?

What if Lazarus could speak? In the traditions of Jewish *midrash* and of feminist biblical interpretation, it is fitting and necessary to let the silenced in the Bible find their voice. What do we imagine Lazarus felt, thought, and knew? What must it have been like to be in a tomb for four days, actually to hear Jesus' voice, to respond, and to be willing to receive a second chance? And then to be immediately thrust into the middle of a religious and political drama that would result in your being simultaneously a local celebrity and hunted down by the religious and political authorities? To lose this friend so soon, who only days earlier had raised you from the dead? To stand by his cross and watch him die, while you were helpless?

And what if you were also secretly—or not so secretly—in love with this friend? And what if you knew *he loved you, too*—that you were "the one whom Jesus loved"? What if Jesus raised Lazarus partly because he could not go through his last weeks without Lazarus's support, company, love, and friendship?

How did the disciples feel about Lazarus's closeness to Jesus in those last weeks? And was Lazarus's identity and memory *erased* from the Gospels of Matthew, Mark, and Luke because of the jealousy of those (Galilean) sources? Or because of overt or covert homophobia?

What was the family structure of Mary, Martha, and Lazarus? In Luke, there is no Lazarus. There are just Mary and Martha. In John 11:2, Mary is the one who says that Lazarus is her brother: "Mary was the one who anointed the Lord with perfume and wiped his feet with her hair; *her brother* Lazarus was ill." What if all three of them were not biological siblings? What if they were siblings in a looser sense? Perhaps they were step-sisters and stepbrothers. Perhaps Martha was a stepsister to both of them.

There are lots of examples, sociologically and historically, of people calling each other relatives when in fact they are not related by blood. During several of the waves of U.S. immigration, people helped each other get into the country by saying that they were relatives when they were not. People often lost contact with their biological families and "adopted" each other as family both to get into the country and to serve as a buffer from this loss, from the isolation and loneliness. Also, in the South and rural areas of the United States, people speak of "shirttail relatives": people who are distantly related in ways much too complicated to figure out. Because of family secrets or scandals, people may not want anyone to find out! So, they're just *relations* in some kind of way. Maybe Jesus was a "shirttail" relative of Mary, Martha, or Lazarus, and that's why it wasn't so scandalous for him to stay at their home. I think of how Native Americans refer to human beings as "all my relations." Remember that John the Baptist was a "shirttail" cousin of Jesus as well. This is a very typical rural understanding of "relations." This was Jesus' style.

Until the 19th and 20th Centuries, the only way in which lesbians ever lived together was by calling themselves "sisters" or "cousins"—and they have, by the millions, over the millennia. Recently, I came home to find a young man doing some repair work on our house. My wife Paula and I do not resemble each other in the slightest. Yet, when I arrived at my home, he said, "Gee, are you and Paula sisters?" He said this because he sensed there was a relationship and because we lived together. Almost every lesbian couple I know gets referred to as "sisters" at some point by people just meeting them. If I had a need to be closeted and if Paula and I had just moved into a new neighborhood, it would be so easy to just say yes to anyone who asked if we were sisters. I've heard of and known many women who have done that. Once that "relationship" is established, who would question it?

When I was at the World Council General Assembly in Australia, MCC folks there organized all the gay and lesbian WCC delegates we could find and then asked for a space in which to hold a worship service. While leaving the assembly site to go to the service, a German woman delegate stopped me and asked if I was going to the service. She had her bicycle with her. I told her yes and that most of those going were gay and lesbian. "No!" she said. And I told her the good news of the Gospel being preached to gays and lesbians and that we had an MCC in Hamburg. She then told me of the underground organization of lesbian pastors in the State Lutheran Church in Germany, called the "Mary and Martha Society." So, obviously, other lesbians have identified with their story as well!

Maybe Mary and Martha weren't a couple. Or maybe they were distant cousins *and* a couple. Maybe Lazarus was Mary's brother, and he was Martha's brother in the same way that Paula views my biological brothers as her own.

Maybe Mary and Martha did live in a little obscure village (in Luke 10) and then moved to Bethany. Or maybe Bethany was their home, but Luke was trying to dissociate them from that rowdy Bethany crowd! (Home of the Lazarus stories, the "beloved disciple" stories, and other "messy" material he would rather not include.)

And what if Mary Magdalene and Mary the *sister of Martha and Lazarus* were the same woman? Many think that Mary Magdalene was a prostitute, although the Bible never says that. We do know that Mary Magdalene had been possessed of "seven demons." She would be labeled mentally ill today. Could it be that her fear and oppression as a lesbian caused her to have symptoms of mental illness, which Jesus healed? Was it possible that they felt safe having Jesus in their home because he knew, and he loved them? The Bible also never mentions Mary Magdalene being married. And it would make sense for her, as a disciple, to be sitting at Jesus' feet and to anoint him—she would be the one who ran to his tomb, who saw him first, and then ran to tell Peter and the "other disciple" (Lazarus, her brother?).

It is amazing how many lesbian women have occupied positions of prestige and importance in little towns and villages all over the world. They were often considered wise spinster women (that is, women who engage in *spinning cloth to make ends meet).* These independent women were teachers, leaders, and healers. Their sexuality was not usually questioned (except in the tragic times of witch hunts). No one thought about them being lesbians, either. They just were. All of us over 40 in the United States grew up knowing such people, who were our parents' ages. And our parents remember them, too, from their childhood. We have always been here, without the labels, closeted and secretive about sexuality. Here were two unmarried women, living together, called "sisters." And, at least sometimes, a brother named Lazarus lived with them. And sometimes a *brother* named Jesus came to stay with them.

Did anyone ever question Jesus' actually staying in a home with two unmarried women and an unmarried brother? Two spinsters and a bachelor brother? Two barren women and a eunuch?

Even the *Anchor Bible Dictionary* notes, "For apparently unmarried women to have received a teacher into their home and engaged him in a dialogue represents an *unusual social situation in first-century Palestine.*"[67]

I had never seen anything close to an adequate treatment of the question of the identity of the beloved disciple until Eller's study. And I feel quite certain that homophobia has contributed a great deal to the lack of desire on the part of mostly male biblical scholars to explore Jesus' special relationship with a particular man. It is interesting to me that Eller can write a whole book on the subject and not even feel that he has to explain away any possible homoerotic possibilities.

This is not, after all, the disciple who *loved Jesus* but the one *whom Jesus loved.* What do we really think of Jesus' having one person in his life whom he loved in a special way? Obviously, he loved the other disciples, his mother, his family, the crowds, and strangers—and even his enemies. Then why mention a *special* or *particular* love in his life? This love must have been different in some sense. One may argue a great deal about whether Jesus may or may not have ever had sexual contact with anyone.

However, if he was *fully human,* he had hormones, sexual organs, and a normal system of sexual arousal. He would have had to have romantic, erotic, or sexual feelings and impulses, whether or not he ever acted on them. How is it possible to read over and over again about this man whom he loved and not imagine that there might have been at least some dimension of passion and eroticism connected to his feelings?

And if gays and lesbians are 10 percent of the population, then 10 percent of Jesus' followers were gay or lesbian. Perhaps 10 percent of the 12 disciples!

I believe that the most obvious way to see Jesus as a sexual being is to see him as bisexual in orientation, if not also in his actions. If our sexuality is most healthy when it is connected, not disconnected, to our values, to intimacy, to our feelings of love and connectedness with others, then the bisexual option sounds the most fair and likely.

I know that saying that Jesus was bisexual in his orientation is really going to send some people into orbit (even some gay and lesbian people)! But *it is very important to de-shame the fact that Jesus, as part of his humanness, part of the concept of incarnation, was sexual.* And this is not a statement about sexual behavior only but about orientation and the erotic, the emotional component of many of his relationships, which may or may not have been overtly or "actively" sexual. To de-shame Jesus' inherent sexuality, to acknowledge that feelings and fantasies were a normal and natural part of his experience of being human, of being male, is one way the Christian church can help begin to de-shame its own members. This *revolutionary* concept that Jesus must have been a sexual being does open the door to speculation about the direction of his sexuality and speculation about his behavior. And opening this door does startle and alarm people, but core Trinitarian theology teaches that Jesus was completely God and completely human.

It does seem as though Jesus is much harder on the sins of hypocrisy, self-righteousness, and greed than he is about breaking sexual morals or laws. He seems frankly a little soft on sexual sins (saying simply, "Go and sin no more" when saving a sexual sinner from the death penalty, meanwhile pointing out everyone's guilt, in John 8). With the possible exception of the teaching on divorce, he doesn't harp on sexuality or sexual sins. Prostitutes loved him. A lot of them still do. They may never trust the church or Christians. But somehow Jesus is a safe, acceptable friend.

I doubt that Jesus consciously knew about the complex psychology (in much debate) of prostitution and its relationship to early childhood sexual trauma. But it is as if he sensed it. He knew not to injure further those who were "sinning," because they were *already* so hurt and broken and hopeless, or shut off from their own self-worth. I know that not all prostitutes see themselves this way. But I do want to make the claim that Jesus' capacity to be compassionate and merciful toward women and men who broke the rules sexually was the result of the facts that he was himself a sexual being, he had been a child and he knew the complexities of love.

7 • Same-Sex Relationships in the Bible

A lesbian hermeneutic moves from deconstruction through suspicion to the constructive tasks of telling the stories of the Bible and "our own stories" with new boldness and a liberating subtext.

There are many important stories in the Bible of persons of the same sex who had passionate, committed, long-lasting relationships. Most of them are just mentioned in passing, or are barely mentioned (the women missionary couples Paul refers to, Paul and Silas, Paul and Barnabas, Paul and Timothy, Paul and John, Mary and Martha, Jesus and the beloved disciple, Jesus and Lazarus—maybe the same couple?). But there are two same-sex couples whose relationships either take center stage in a biblical drama, or whose relationships are the main subject of a biblical drama: David and Jonathan (in 1 Samuel), and Ruth and Naomi (in the Book of Ruth).

Saul, Jonathan, David

Jesus Christ is called by Christians the "Son of David" because King David became the *model* for Messianic hopes. If we think of Jesus as bisexual in orientation (while bypassing speculation on how he lived for the moment), this certainly makes sense, as David is probably the most clearly bisexual figure in the whole Bible.

The authors or editors of 1 and 2 Samuel really must have been palace insiders. They have incredible insight, palace gossip, and details about the early kings of Israel especially. The stories, in particular those of Saul, Jonathan, David and his sons, read like a Greek tragedy. I think the writers were possibly palace eunuchs, those invisible officials and servants who always had their ears to the wall and their mouths shut. Also, 1 Samuel's account of the triangle among Saul, Jonathan, and David is filled with homoeroticism. And the descriptions of David physically are among the only descriptions of their kind in the whole Bible. They stand out for that reason. The author was very attuned to David's ample beauty.

Tom Horner, in his book *Jonathan Loved David,* was really the first to make this case. He does so primarily from a literary, critical, and historical point of view.

The David and Jonathan stories contained in 1 Samuel chapters 18 to 25 are among the oldest writing in the Old Testament. They were written in much the same way that classical Greek history was written. The stories are ones of "warrior lovers," common in the Ancient Near East. In patriarchal cultures, men and women lived separately. All men, whatever their sexuality, were expected to marry and have children. But many men also engaged in homosexual sex—some occasionally, some regularly. Some of these men were bisexual, and some were more serious and romantic about their male lovers than about their wives or female lovers.

The concept of warrior lovers was considered noble and normal. The adventure and *glamor* (a gay sexual word, actually)[68] of going to war was viewed erotically. And there was no shame connected to homoeroticism. The only shame might be if you wanted to get really serious about a male lover for life. That was considered *feminizing,* and was to be avoided. Male, "boys-will-be-boys" homoeroticism was normal and fun, but not to be overly celebrated or acknowledged. This is still true in many cultures today.

David's classic beauty first attracted Saul in 1 Samuel 16:4–23. It says that "Saul loved him greatly" and that David's musical abilities calmed and relieved Saul. It would not have been unthinkable for Saul to have been intimate with David as young man. In any case, it eventually became a tragic triangle. David had actually already been secretly anointed by Samuel to replace Saul as king. Saul began to get jealous of David. To make matters worse, Saul's son Jonathan, who was supposed to succeed him as king, was totally smitten with David and wanted David to succeed his father. This meant that Jonathan was playing the more passive role in this romance, even to the point of giving up his crown for David (1 Samuel 18:1–4; 20:30–34).

This, of course, infuriated Saul all the more. The account of Jonathan's first meeting with David could hardly be more explicitly homoerotic:

> When David had finished speaking to Saul, the soul of Jonathan was bound to the soul of David, and Jonathan loved him as his own soul. Saul took him that day and would not let him

return to his father's house. Then Jonathan made a covenant with David, because he loved him as his own soul. Jonathan stripped himself of the robe he was wearing and gave it to David, and his armor, and even his sword and his bow and his belt. (1 Samuel 18:1–4)

Tom Horner documents how this account compares with similar kinds of relationships described in Greek literature in particular and how it compares to classic homoerotic warrior literature. Jonathan's stripping of his robes and armor may be a sign of sexual as well as political submission, something that must have infuriated Saul. Tom Horner details all the correspondences in the story of Jonathan and David linguistically and literarily with other homoerotic literature.[69]

I think it is amazing that the original *Oxford Annotated Bible* comment on this passage says only, "A deep friendship arose between David and Jonathan."[70] The third edition keeps it toned down as well, saying, "*Loved* implies political loyalty in addition to personal affection." Ah, yes! Very deep.

Saul is extremely threatened both by David's success as a warrior and his relationship with his son. The NRSV, in its annotation to 1 Samuel 20:1–42, notes that this passage is "an independent tradition of the break between Saul and David, incompatible with much of Chapter 19. David is represented as still a member of the king's household, and Jonathan seems unaware of Saul's hatred of David. The break between Saul and David was so significant that many different stories about it were told."[71] And I think some of the "different" accounts are told from the *insiders'* point of view, and these are the ones that have the romantic, sexual dimensions.

In one account of the conflict between David and Saul, David tells Jonathan, "Your father wants to kill me." Jonathan says, "No, it can't be true," and then betrays his father to help save his beloved (and the future king of Israel). David gives Jonathan an out, saying, "If you don't want to betray your father, just kill me!" Jonathan is grieved by the suggestion and then makes a "sacred covenant" with him, which includes these words:

> "If I am alive, show me the faithful love of the Lord; but if I die, never *cut off* your faithful love from my house, even if the Lord is to *cut off* every one of the enemies of David from the face of the earth." Thus Jonathan made a covenant with the house of

David, saying, "May the Lord seek out the enemies of David."
Jonathan made David swear again by his love for him; for he
loved him as he loved his own life. *1 Samuel 20:14–17*

Notice the use of the term "cut off" and how Jonathan's request is to
be included in David's family eternally. Jonathan wants his eternal life
to be connected to David's family and his descendants. It is amazing to
me that most biblical scholars cannot even bear to think of this relationship
as homoerotic. I have seen a few notes and comments that were actually
apologetic: "Well, we know this sounds awfully homosexual, but it just
can't be. It can't be because David, the greatest king of Israel, the forerun-
ner of the Messiah, could not have been *queer!*" Actually, David seems very
bisexual in his romantic interests. It is possible that Jonathan was more
truly gay and more in love with David than David was with Jonathan. After
all, David needed Jonathan's help. There follows, in 1 Samuel 20:35–42, a
very intimate account of another secret meeting. It says, in part:

David rose from beside the stone heap and prostrated himself
with his face on the ground. He bowed three times, and they
kissed each other, and wept with each other. David wept the
more. *1 Samuel 20:41*

There is no comment at all on this verse in the NRSV. The note to
"David wept the more" says, *"Meaning of Hebrew uncertain."* In the old RSV
it says, "Until David recovered himself." In another note, it says that the
literal meaning is possibly "David exceeded himself." Others say that
it may mean he was "overcome." Overcome? With feeling? Passion? Tom
Horner says this may be a euphemism for sexual arousal.

In any case, if this had been an encounter between a man and a
woman, scholars would not hesitate to acknowledge and write about this
most explicit of romantic and sexual relationships. Even the new *Anchor
Bible Dictionary* homophobically refuses to entertain any possibility that
David and Jonathan's friendship was also homoerotic. As if, of course,
homosexuality would make it bad, dirty, and not about *friendship*. As if
intimate same-gender couples are not friends.

In addition, there is an incredible section of the narrative in which
Jonathan is questioned by Saul about David's whereabouts. Saul realizes
that Jonathan is covering for David and curses Jonathan's mother and says
he should be ashamed of his relationship with David. Saul, in his own

homophobia and denial, sees his son as the more "passive" partner in this romance because of Jonathan's submission to David and to David's agenda, and he is trying to humiliate Jonathan about it. Jonathan's response is to get up from the table in anger and go to his room and not to eat for two days because he is grieved for David and because his father has disgraced him (1 Samuel 20:30–34). How clear can it be? Anyone who has ever come out to his or her parents knows about these scenes! Saul blames Jonathan's mother, and Jonathan pouts in his room while lovesick over David.

King David, as a young warrior, was the love of Prince Jonathan's life. Centuries of homophobic Bible commentaries have kept them in the closet too long!

But just in case you still have any doubt, here is the clearest evidence. It is David's lament for Saul and Jonathan, both killed in battle:

> Saul and Jonathan, beloved and lovely!
> In life and in death they were not divided;
> they were swifter than eagles,
> they were stronger than lions. . . .
> How the mighty have fallen
> in the midst of the battle!
> Jonathan lies slain upon your high places.
> I am distressed for you, my brother Jonathan;
> greatly beloved were you to me; your love to me was wonderful,
> passing the love of women. *2 Samuel 1:23, 25–26*

The third edition of the *Oxford Annotated Bible* discounts these verses: "passing the love of women expresses the closeness of David's relationship to Jonathan but does not necessarily imply a sexual relationship" [page 448]. This is progress from the first edition that made no mention of this passage at all.

If this had been a love poem from a woman to a man or a man to a woman, it would be noted. (Such as, "Gloria, Gloria, I am distressed for you; greatly beloved were you to me; your love was wonderful, passing the love of [those other] women!") Also, David here acknowledges his feeling of love for women (plural), and we surely have stories about David and heterosexual lust (Bathsheba). It seems too much to believe that David is not speaking here of his passionate, sexual feelings for Jonathan. If it were about a nonsexual friendship, then David would have spoken about how this love was special and *different* from his love for women. Instead he says his wonderful feeling of love for Jonathan, and Jonathan's love for him, *passes* or *surpasses* the love of women. He is *comparing similar kinds of love*, not contrasting them. Also note that the lament shifts at the end: the verses switch from the third person to the first person.

Then there is David's grief for Saul, mentor, king, benefactor, and possibly also lover. We must remember that, with an understanding of warrior lovers, this would not have been scandalous and would not have impaired Saul's heterosexual image one bit. The depth of denial in Bibles, commentaries, and dictionaries about David and Jonathan is only one more clear indication of the depth of the homophobia in our history and culture.

Ruth and Naomi

David and Jonathan are one example of same-sex, lifelong relationships in the Bible. The other remarkable same-sex couple consists of Ruth and Naomi. Both of these couples provide the Bible's most moving models of committed love under stressful circumstances. In fact, of course, Ruth is actually King David's great-great-grandmother. Maybe homosexuality *is* genetic—at least in the Bible!

The book of Ruth is really a romantic novella. In this story, Naomi, her husband, and sons move to Moab because of famine, and then her husband and sons die. Naomi's sons have married Moabite women. Now she is widowed with no heir—*cut off*. Her daughters-in-law, Ruth and Orpah, both love her. Naomi decides to go back to Palestine and encourages her daughters-in-law to return to their own kinfolk.

They are both reluctant to leave their beloved mother-in-law. Remember that, in their cultures, women were segregated socially from men, so the women of the family were very close. They want to stay with Naomi, but she tells them she can't help them. Even if she were to remarry, she is too old to produce sons, much less sons for them to marry!

Orpah returns to her family, but not Ruth. It says that "Ruth clung to her" (Ruth 1:4). Then Ruth makes this moving vow (used for millennia in heterosexual wedding ceremonies):

> Do not press me to leave you
> or to turn from following you!

> Where you go I will go;
> Where you lodge I will lodge;
> Your people shall be my people,
> and your God my God.
> Where you die, I will die—
> there I will be buried.
> May the Lord do thus and so to me, and more as well
> if even death parts me from you! *Ruth 1:16–17*

Ruth returns to Bethlehem with Naomi. There, as two impoverished *barren* widows (one a foreigner), they glean in the fields of Naomi's cousin Boaz. (Another "shirttail relative" story!) Ruth then sexually seduces Boaz and manipulates him into marrying her. He has no obligation legally to do this, because, although he is Naomi's kin, he is *not* responsible for Ruth. He is not *her* kin. But of course, Ruth and Naomi have a covenant and are *family*. Boaz is an honorable man, accepts responsibility for his "kinswoman," and marries Ruth.

There is never any remote suggestion of romance between Ruth and Boaz.[72] Boaz represents male privilege and is a benign figure. This novella is told very much from a woman's point of view.[73] Boaz is a *"means to an end,"* the end being survival. Eventually, Ruth has a son. The novella ends happily with these words:

> Then the women said to Naomi, "Blessed be the Lord, who has not left you this day without next-of-kin; and may his name be renowned in Israel! He shall be to you a restorer of life and a nourisher of your old age; for your daughter-in-law *who loves* you, who is more to you *than seven sons,* has borne him." Then Naomi took the child and laid him in her bosom, and became his nurse. The women of the neighborhood gave him a name, saying, "a son has been born to Naomi." They named him Obed; he became the father of Jesse, the father of David. *Ruth 4:14–17—emphasis is the author's*

The women of the neighborhood give Boaz absolutely no role and recognition in this. They name the baby and say Ruth is more to Naomi than *seven sons*. Ruth takes the role of husband and of son to Naomi, by *giving* her a son. She uses Boaz to do it, but Ruth's is the active role: she is the *hero* of the story. And Naomi is really the subject, the main character. Ruth is Naomi's *redeemer,* providing her with a child to care for her in her old age, preventing her from being *cut off.*

Clearly Ruth and Naomi's relationship is unusual and unique. The women in the neighborhood recognize it and admire, even envy, it. They are boasting about this woman who is worth more than seven sons. Ruth and Naomi act like a couple. Nowhere have I ever seen biblical commentators talk about the sex-role reversals, how the story plays off the traditional gender roles, or about the remarkable statement of committed love, *unto death do us part,* from one woman to another.

This is particularly significant in light of the way in which mother-in-law/daughter-in-law relationships are viewed in white Western culture. Mother-in-law jokes are common. Often, mothers are considered to be in *rivalry* with their daughters-in-law for their sons' attention or with their sons-in-law for their daughters' attention. The idea that a mother and daughter-in-law could have a deep love and friendship is remarkable. It is a *subversive* aspect of the text. The only acknowledgment of this I have read is in Mary Hunt's book *A Fierce Tenderness,*[74] or any acknowledgment of the *subversion* of male privilege and power in this story. Ruth gets what she and Naomi need from the system to survive: a husband and a son. But this is all done in the context of a women's community, where Ruth and Naomi are the central relationship.

Is it possible that Ruth and Naomi were also an intimate couple? Perhaps Ruth was not really Naomi's daughter-in-law but an unmarried woman or widow who befriended Naomi. Maybe they made up the story about Ruth being her daughter-in-law in order to protect their relationship. *It's been done many, many times by lesbians who needed to lie to protect their secret.* In their case, it was necessary for Ruth to be eligible to marry Boaz—Naomi's cousin, not Ruth's. Perhaps they *were* mother and daughter-in-law, but Ruth fell in love with Naomi. They could have had a deep platonic friendship that was also romantic in a homoerotic but not homosexual way. Many lesbians never had the freedom, courage, or opportunity to have a sexual relationship with another woman, though all their desires and fantasies were homosexual. Many women throughout history lived with a "roommate" all their lives in committed, faithful "Boston marriages," without daring to be sexual.[75] The fact that no biblical commentators have been willing to explore the meanings of these same-sex friendships, romances, or relationships is powerful evidence of the overwhelmingly negative politics of biblical interpretation at work. In a culture that vilifies homosexuals as promiscuous, as unable to keep commitments, as faithless, these stories of committed faithful love, filled with risk taking, are moving, powerful biblical stories for gay and lesbian people. We must take them back.

The fact that there is not *one* example in the Bible of heterosexuals who express their undying commitment to each other in a way that can be used in heterosexual marriage ceremonies is certainly a major omission! Heterosexuals have ripped off our love stories for too long! I find myself fantasizing about going through every wedding liturgy in every Christian worship book with my scissors and cutting out Ruth's words to Naomi. *You can't steal them!*

Colette Jackson and I performed her play, *Bibles and Bulldaggers*, based on my queer interpretation of the Bible, at Highways Performance Space in Santa Monica in June of 1994. After the first or second performance, a young heterosexual couple came up to me shyly, saying how much they loved the play, especially the part about Ruth and Naomi—which I had explained in the talk-back with the audience afterward. They liked the passage from Ruth so much that they wanted my permission to use it in their wedding ceremony! I was so touched I almost started laughing, but I quite seriously gave them permission, but only if somehow they could indicate that these words were originally spoken from one woman to another. They cheerfully agreed to my "terms," thanked me, and left. I have fantasies of interrupting poor, unsuspecting heterosexuals at their wedding with "STOP, in the name of Ruth and Naomi, Jonathan and David! Stop stealing our stories while making our relationships illegal or characterizing them as immoral!"

More Gays and Lesbians in the Bible

Is that all there is? A couple dozen eunuchs strategically placed; barren women; Mary, Martha, Lazarus, and the beloved disciple; the wise men; and two famous same-sex couples? That's a good start, but I think there are a lot more. It is as if *they* keep appearing and appearing. The more we ask questions, challenge heterosexual assumptions, the more we see them emerge from ancient biblical closets.

What, for instance, do we think of Lydia in Acts 16:11–15? It is interesting that in this story the narration of the book of Acts moves to the first-person plural, which means the author may have joined the missionary group on its way to Philippi. Lydia is reported in this story to be a wealthy, independent businesswoman. She owns a home large enough to house the apostle Paul and his friends. No husband is mentioned. She is someone who worships God, and she is either a Jew from the city of Thyatira (in what is now Turkey), a Gentile convert to Judaism, or a Gentile "God-fearer." Apparently there were not enough Jewish men to have a minyan on the Sabbath at the outdoor synagogue, but she assembles a group of God-fearing women to hear Paul.

Lydia becomes the first European Christian, and, when she is converted, all her household is baptized. This makes her the equivalent of a *pater-* (or in her case, *mater-*) *familias,* the head of a household, which as a woman was unusual. The new church in Philippi begins to meet in her house (Acts 16:40). Lydia has gone against Jewish customs not only by speaking to Paul in public but by inviting him to speak to this group of women and then inviting him into her house.[76] In addition, Lydia's business is quite interesting. She is a seller of purple dye. Purple, of course, has ancient associations with magic, royalty, and gays and lesbians. The dye was made from certain mollusks. Homer, in the Iliad, mentions two *women* who were famous for the art of purple dyeing in Lydia (a city in Asia Minor), founders of a tradition of women makers and sellers of purple dye.[77] Lydia, the woman, was an inheritor of this tradition described by Homer.

I also had fun with Bible maps on this one! Did you know that the Isle of Lesbos does appear on every biblical map of Paul's travels? Lesbos had been home to the greatest lesbian poet of the Ancient Near East, Sappho, in the seventh century B.C. If you draw a straight line from Thyatira (where Lydia was from) to Philippi in Macedonia (where she met Paul), you will draw it right through the Isle of Lesbos! Perhaps Lydia had stopped at Lesbos on her way to Philippi. I wonder if the legendary two women who originated purple dye knew of Sappho. What might they have known of what was called *Sapphic love?* Is there some kind of women's tradition, or lesbian tradition, going on here that is only hinted at by Homer and in the Bible?

Paul himself actually stopped on the Isle of Lesbos once! In the Bible it is called Mitylene (the name of the capital city of the island). Acts 20:4 records this. I wonder if the name was changed in order to suppress the association of Lesbos with women who loved women?

It is not clear whether or not women like Lydia would have known about Sappho or her lesbian community, named after the island on which they lived. What part of that Sapphic women's culture still existed, aboveground or underground, in New Testament times in Lesbos, or Greece, or anywhere?

Uppity Women

It also seems to me that Jesus was often drawn to women who challenged him, who talked back to him, who were outside the ordinary social rules.

According to the story in John 2, Mary pressed her son Jesus to do something about their relatives who had no more wine for the wedding feast. Jesus (a little curtly, I think) told her that this was not the time for him to be showing off his Messianic powers. She ignored him and told the servants to "do what Jesus told them." She was pushy. Jesus responded by doing what his mother wanted; he fixed the problem (John 2:5–11).

Two chapters later, he meets a lone Samaritan woman at Jacob's well. There, he engages in a theological dialogue with a woman who is clearly a sexual outcast. She's had five husbands and lived with a man who was not her husband in a small rural village. How many times a day, do you suppose, people called her the equivalent of "whore" and "slut"? While she was not a lesbian, she was a woman who broke the rules, sexually. According to Jewish law, Jesus should not have engaged her in conversation, because she was a woman, a Samaritan, and a slut! But he asks her for a drink, engages her not only in small talk but asks about her personal life, and talks about theology. She talks back to him. He touches her spiritually and probably emotionally. He does not judge her or call her anything. He treats her respectfully, as if she has valuable thoughts. What adult man, do you suppose, had ever treated her this way? (John 4:7–44)

Not only that but, after the disciples showed up, the Scriptures say that they couldn't believe he was talking to the woman, but they don't dare question him. Why not? What didn't they want to hear?

Then, they actually stay in this village for a few days. The Samaritan woman's outcast status is transformed as she becomes the center of attention in a positive way. She becomes the first apostle of the good news of Jesus recorded in the Gospel of John. Jesus meets with many of these villagers, who actually believe her story about her experience with Jesus.

Where do you suppose he and the disciples stay? What were the results of their visit? When Jesus left, did the villages still care how many husbands she had had?

In the Gospel of Luke (chapter 8:40–48), a woman who has been hemorrhaging for 12 years attempts to be healed by *unobtrusively* touching the hem of Jesus' garment. She does this, but Jesus is affected by her gesture. He describes it as "power going forth" from him. She has taken her healing from him, without his consent. Instead of being angry or feeling deceived or even *violated,* Jesus expresses awe and admiration for this woman's aggressive seeking of God's healing through him. The fact is that, by touching a Jewish male while bleeding, she is making him ritually unclean. It is never clear to me whether or not Jesus abided by the law or not when he was touched by menstruating women or lepers or anyone "unclean." He would have been required to go through a process of ritual cleansing. It sounds as though, when it came to healing, he did not keep these laws, any more than he kept the Sabbath laws. In any case, he showed encouragement and admiration for women who *took what they wanted from him.*

The most glaring example of this is his encounter with the Syro-Phoenician woman, recorded with some differences in Mark 7:24–30 and Matthew 15:21–28. Here, as Jesus is attempting to get away from the crowds, this Greek (or Canaanite) woman finds him. In all fairness, the guy could *never* get a vacation or be left alone. In Matthew's version, he refuses to speak to her at all at first. Finally, she is being such a pest that the disciples beg him to see her. Jesus then hears that her little daughter is possessed by a demon. Jesus refused to heal her at first, saying that he has come to the "lost house of Israel" and is not open to helping *her kind* of people. But she will not give up. Even if he was elitist, racist—even if she despised him—she would not give up for the sake of her daughter. So it says she kneels before him, even after he rejects her, and begs him to heal her daughter. She talks back. She is aggressive, persistent, and will endure any shame from Jesus to save her child, including his saying, "Let the children [Israel] be fed, for it is not right to take the children's bread and throw it to the dogs [Gentiles, Canaanites?]" (Mark 7:27).

Now, at this point, I might have thought of some snappy rejoinder to that *dogs* remark and marched out of there. "Bitch! Are you calling me a bitch? I'll show you what a bitch I am!" But this woman is as single-minded as it is possible to be. She responds to him *from the social position of a dog* with relentless determination and says, "Sir, even the dogs under the table eat the children's crumbs" (Mark 7:28).

Jesus then says, "For *saying that,* you may go—the demon has left your daughter" (Mark 7:29).

Jesus took no credit for a lot of the miracles that involved uppity women. He was almost a passive participant, a reluctant bystander to their process of claiming and receiving what they needed. It is interesting, though, that he would say, "For saying that ..." Is that because she is like the woman who pesters the unjust judge "until she gets what she wants" (Luke 18:1–8)? Was Jesus rewarding her for her persistence, her refusal to back down? Was he simply in touch with what God had done, as she exercised her own faith by pestering him? Was he touched by the way in which she endured his abuse and then turned it around, perhaps hoping to humble him with her willingness to bear any abuse for her daughter's sake? He never claimed to heal her daughter. He announced the healing. This uppity foreign woman got his attention.

Luke, a more Gentile Gospel, does not record this story. The Palestinian Gospels have it—perhaps showing a developmental issue in Jesus' ministry—that he did not start out with an openness to Gentiles, women or men, even though Luke might want us to believe that.

In any case, women are touched and healed by him (sometimes) almost in spite of him, and he seems very attracted to uppity women who talk back. What kind of man would be attracted to such women?

The Lost Coin

For a more fanciful gay and lesbian exegesis, I like the parable of the woman who lost a coin and then finds it (Luke chapters 8–10). In a trinity of parables, Jesus chooses a shepherd, a woman (there is no mention of a husband—the story reads as if she is alone in her house), and a father to represent the God who seeks and finds the lost. The shepherd and the prodigal stories are the ones that we generally hear about in sermons. Jesus' image of God as a woman who has lost her coin gets precious little attention.

In this simple parable, a woman has ten silver coins, loses one, lights a lamp, and searches for it, sweeping the house, until she finds it. When she finds it, she calls together her friends and neighbors to rejoice. It is interesting that, in this case, the lost coin represents her security and well-being in a culture in which women who were alone, barren, or widowed were always vulnerable. Money, any savings, would be her only hope in this case, and finding the coin is saving herself, perhaps even more directly than in the story about the shepherd or the father.

I wonder if Jesus was conscious of choosing a woman for this parable about a lost coin because its value would be greater to her than to a man in a patriarchal society. Perhaps he knew the politics of this situation would heighten the pathos of losing and finding a coin. It is this woman's independence and power that are at stake here, a point lost on male Bible commentators and preachers for most of 2,000 years.

I am fascinated by the fact that there are ten coins. In one sense, a *tithe* has been lost. Gays and lesbians are about 10 percent of every population. Are we actually a tithe of humanity? Is there an economy in the creation of human beings that reserves 10 percent of us to be available in every "tribe" to exercise our particular tribal gifts? Are we a *lost coin* that God is joyfully *finding* and lifting up in our day? Isn't God thrilled that the gay and lesbian children are being found? Isn't there rejoicing in heaven over that (if not at the National Council of Churches of Christ or in evangelical TV programs such as "The 700 Club")? In a similar metaphor, are we not that *pinch of leaven* in the *loaf* of every culture? A necessary, particular ingredient?

The Gay Centurion

Tom Horner has documented the gay associations with the healing of the centurion's slave in Matthew 8:5–13 (and also in Luke 7:1–10).[78] The story is about a prominent centurion, loved by the Jews in his town, a supporter of the synagogue, who comes out to meet Jesus and plead that he will save his servant's life. In the version told in Matthew, the Greek term used for servant is different from the term used in Luke. The term in Matthew is one that was associated with a common practice among Gentiles in Jesus' time: he was a "slave boy," which meant a young male lover, who might have been a debt slave.[79]

This relationship was common among Roman soldiers and would *not* have meant that the centurion was not also married. It would have been odd for the centurion to go personally to Jesus to plead for the life of a servant, even one who was "dear to him." The story makes more sense (and is more poignant) if this is a more intimate relationship. In the Gospel of John 4, there is a similar story about a "royal official" who pleads for the life of his son. The annotation in the NRSV says he is a "Gentile military officer" (another *eunuch?*).[80] This story is connected in the annotations to the other two in Matthew and Luke. It was the custom of Romans to adopt slaves as their sons when they were emancipated, especially slaves held in high regard or slaves who had also been lovers. This may be the same event reported differently in Matthew, Luke, and John. What is interesting is Jesus' nonjudgmental approach to this centurion's pain and love relationship. As Matthew 8:10 reports it, "When Jesus heard him, he was amazed and said to those who followed him, 'Truly I tell you, in no one in Israel have I found such faith.'"

Women Partners in the New Testament

Women scholars are beginning to explore the patterns and possibilities of women partners in the New Testament, using Adrienne Rich's "continuum" concept of lesbian relationships. One such "couple" consists of *Tryphaena and Tryphosa,* mentioned by Paul in Romans 16:12. These are both Greek women's names. Also, *Euodia and Syntyche* are mentioned in Philippians 4:2; they were apparently having a conflict that was affecting their ministry partnership.[81] Did the bias against heterosexual marriage among religious leaders select for gay and lesbian leadership in the early church? The celibate priesthood and the requirements for celibacy among the Roman Catholic religious has certainly selected for a higher percentage of gays and lesbians than the usual 10 percent. Many of these leaders are not celibate, as is becoming clearer through the incidence of AIDS and the coming-out stories of priests and nuns.

What About Paul?

Early Christianity would have attracted anyone who felt like an outsider. Paul fits the profile of a hyper-perfectionist trying to change his own sexual orientation. Before his conversion, he tries to prove himself by persecuting those at the edge. After his conversion, he proves himself by throwing himself into reaching the outsiders of early Christianity—the Gentiles.

Bishop John Shelby Spong, in *Rescuing the Bible from Fundamentalism,*[82] makes one of the more uncompromising cases for Paul's homosexuality. It does seem as though Paul has very little compassion or patience for those who are "troubled" by heterosexual lust. It is as if he cannot comprehend why some of the men have to marry, although he acknowledges that it is "better to marry than to be aflame with passion" (1 Corinthians 7:9). Paul continuously has fights and emotional scenes with his male traveling companions. Clearly, Paul is happy to travel with men and often stays in the homes of wealthy, *independent* (lesbian?) women.

It is clear that Paul sees himself as a celibate, perhaps an *asexual* person. But his temperament, his emotional preference, seems to be toward men. If being gay or lesbian is not so much about behavior but about a matrix of feelings, behavior, and culture, Paul may have been a repressed, closeted (even to himself?) homosexual.

The Color Purple

One of the key women in Paul's world was Lydia, the dyer of purple. As we have seen, there are interesting connections to the color purple in the Ancient Near East and in the Bible. Judy Grahn was the first to document seriously the extensive connections of the color purple to ancient concepts of magic, spirituality, transformation, change, royalty, spiritual power, and gays and lesbians.[83] If these connections are accurate historically and in terms of mythology and ancient symbolism, then what *is* the relationship of the color purple in the Bible to all these issues? At minimum, we know that purple cloth is associated with the Temple and Jesus wore the color purple to the cross.

What difference does it make to see the Bible in this way? I believe that it is essential for gay men, lesbians, and bisexuals to take back the Bible. If we are not included among the stories and characters of the Bible, then it cannot be our book. It is also important for heterosexuals not to see the Bible monolithically either, but to see the people of the Bible as they must have been: as varied and complex in their sexuality as human beings are today.

Years from now, none of this will be shocking or unusual. Biblical annotations will include footnotes about us, and not just in a negative way. More biblical commentaries and dictionaries will contain articles by feminists, gays, lesbians, and others doing important work in previously unexplored areas of the Bible and human sexuality. As gay and lesbian biblical scholars come out, do the scholarship, and pay the price, the texts will be healed. Meanwhile, we must boldly begin to ask the questions, make suggestions, and "go too far."

Seismic Theology

For a large number of people, accepting that there are queer people in the Bible will be an earth-shattering experience—a theological earthquake. God's role in what are geological and theological events must be looked at in the context of biblical and modern views of God's relationship to nature and natural disasters and can help us all construct a biblical theology that reflects God's creativity and our human diversity.

For many people at MCC Los Angeles, the earthquake in 1994 that destroyed our building became a fundamental faith crisis. If we cannot count on God to keep the earth from shaking or to keep our church building standing upright or our homes or lives from being destroyed, what can we count on God for, anyway? I remember reading Paul Tillich's theology in seminary. He wrote about a God who is the "ground of our being." What happens to our faith in the ground of our being when the *ground* is shaking?! Tillich obviously had a seismically insensitive theology!

This faith crisis was acted out in many ways in our church. People who believed they had long ago left behind the *judging* God suddenly found themselves wondering if God were exercising a fundamentalist-style micro-justice in toppling a gay-and-lesbian-owned church building. There was almost a kind of morbid glee when our members learned that other predominantly *straight* churches had been destroyed, too! What a relief, we weren't *singled out!* Other members found themselves still unable to return to church.

An African-American member of my church talked poignantly about how, in the African-American community, church has always been the "safe place." For many African Americans (and for poor folk of different ethnic backgrounds), the church was sometimes the only piece of real estate they ever owned or hoped to own. MCC, like the historic black church, is the "historic" church of the gay and lesbian community. For African Americans, the church was, and sometimes still is, everything; it was where community meetings were held (when they couldn't meet legally in other buildings). It was *theirs;* no one could take it away from them. It was where they discussed voting and politics; it housed the burial societies; it was a place where you could always get help. African-American gays and lesbians at MCC Los Angeles had a different historical perspective, a different lens, perhaps a more intense spiritual and political symbolic investment in the church building than other members. Church structures are not *supposed* to fall down. If *they* fall down, the community is *exposed* and vulnerable in devastating ways.

MCC Los Angeles members who owned their own homes generally did not take the destruction of the church so personally, unless they were African-American or had other complicating issues. Thus, the destruction of our building challenged our multicultural community in new ways. We had to communicate more in order to understand each other's particular pains and sorrows.

Latinos and Latinas had yet other concerns. Many of them are immigrants from countries that experience devastating earthquakes, where there was little money for the kinds of seismic preparedness that had been possible in Los Angeles. They had been through experiences where hundreds and even thousands had died in similar earthquakes. They *knew* not to trust the ground. They, of all groups in Los Angeles, took the longest time to reenter their homes, even if they had not had any damage. It took some of the Hispanic members of MCC Los Angeles a very long time to come back to church with any sense of safety, if they ever could. On top of the lack of safety in a culture that is increasingly anti-immigrant, now not even the church was a safe place.

Race, culture, and class privileges made the earthquake less traumatic for some than for others. But even the *most* privileged among us knew that all the retrofitting, all the money and power and education in the world, amounted to *nothing* in comparison to the force of this event. For most of us, it was the most powerful external physical force we had ever experienced.

I am still sometimes haunted by a memory of the aftermath of the Mexico City earthquake in 1985. One of our church members was killed, and others saw death and injuries on a scale from which they have never quite been able to recover. A few days after the quake, we had an ant attack in our kitchen, as happens in Los Angeles when the weather is very dry. The sight of thousands of ants crawling over the kitchen counter repulsed me, as it does many people. I grabbed the bug spray and began to kill them. Suddenly I realized that, for *them,* this was a terrible disaster—a lot like an earthquake or flood, perhaps. I felt helpless and horrible. I did not want to feel this connection *at all.* I wanted to dissociate from these tiny creatures, from any sense of their world or existence. They were in my way. I could so easily regard them as nonlife, to be disposed of at my will, disregarded. I wanted so much *not* to feel it, not to connect them to the human beings in Mexico, to my own humanness, to my own existence and stark vulnerability as a *life form*. It infuriated me that I could not close my mind to these thoughts, and I felt just a little *mad* for a while. I felt grief and shame and helplessness. For a long while, I tried other ant control methods, some of which I still use, such as keeping little pans of water outside the house, outside doors and windows near their entry points. This seemed to help, at least for a while.

A big picture and a very tiny picture intersected at that moment in a powerful way for me. What about our human desire to control and exploit life? Does all life have inalienable rights? When we speak of reverence for life as a value, what kind of life are we talking about? What are the limits, if any? What do I do with all that bug spray? (It is probably bad for the ozone layer anyway!) How far do I have to go in sharing the planet, and with which species?

The Bible and Earthquakes

There are about 25 references to earthquakes in the Bible. Some of these references are not necessarily *theological* at all, as in this reference from the first verse of the first chapter of Amos:

> The words of Amos, who was among the shepherds of Tekoa, which he saw concerning Israel in the days of King Uzziah of Judah and in the days of King Jeroboam, son of Joash of Israel, two years before the earthquake. *Amos 1:1*

The earthquake. Zechariah mentions the very same earthquake in 14:5, as if all persons reading this will simply know or remember a particular earthquake called "the earthquake." Anyone alive and near Los Angeles on January 17, 1994, will remember *the* earthquake. Until, of course, something greater in our disaster memory replaces it as a dating device. The earthquake during Amos's lifetime must have had devastating effects to be so singularly remembered. The *Oxford Annotated Bible* simply comments, "The earthquake, mentioned again in Zechariah 4:5, cannot be precisely dated." The time came when the memory faded and life went on. Sometimes earthquakes, then, are simply recorded as an alternative method of dating a person or events.

There are two categories of the *theological* uses of earthquakes in Scripture. One category I would call *earthquakes as evidence of God's self-expression*.

Sometimes earthquakes (accompanied by wind or fire or even sheer *silence)* are a metaphor for the theophany of God: how God's presence is experienced by humans. This occurs on Mount Sinai (Numbers 16:31–34) and is frequently the case in the Psalms. Earthquakes are also described as the "earth's trembling response to the power of God's presence" (or appearance). This is not the same as the use of earthquakes as an expression of divine wrath—an idea that is alive and well in our times! The book of Revelation is filled with references to violent earthquakes that sometimes kill thousands of people, which is part of an overall apocalyptic vision of the judgment of God upon the wicked. There are hints of this in the "little apocalypses" of Matthew and Luke, including references to earthquakes.

Sometimes just the power and force of the divine, without any particularly negative associations, are viewed as the cause of earthquakes, or earthquakes are interpreted as being motivated by a particular event that has angered God or as signs of God's total, *generic* anger at human beings.

Biblical earthquake theologies don't end here, however; it is even more complicated than that. Earthquakes also seem to play a role in *events related to divine intervention* or that support the divine plan. In one case, an earthquake accompanies Jonathan's (a gay man's?) victory over the Philistines, increasing the "panic in their camp" (1 Samuel chapters 14 and 15).

In the New Testament, in Matthew's Gospel only, earthquakes accompany both the crucifixion and the resurrection of Jesus. In the account of the resurrection (Matthew 28:2), it is an earthquake that actually rolls the stone away from Jesus' tomb! The *elemental forces* of the universe are called to play a part in this cosmic drama of the death and resurrection of God's anointed. One may wonder if earthquakes were very frequent in those years or if those particular earthquakes would provide dating corroboration for the events. Was this earthquake simply inserted as a literary device meant to heighten the drama of the events or to connect them theologically to God's theophany, God's anger, or to the apocalyptic view of Jesus' life and ministry? Are the mentions of earthquakes incidental to those events, or do they carry more meaning than most scholars have been willing to explore? Are they a part of the backdrop or a component of the events themselves?

Perhaps my favorite earthquake story in the Bible is in Acts 16, the story of Paul and Silas and the jailer. This new movement was hardly a church yet. Those early followers of the Way were adventurous, and totally committed to sharing the life-giving, healing grace of God in Jesus Christ. They lived and died to do this.

Paul and Silas are in Philippi, where they meet Lydia (the seller of purple, you will recall). The women in her prayer group, and apparently some men, are now a part of the church in Lydia's house (Acts 16).

Inevitably, Paul and Silas run into some legal trouble. A slave woman, who the Scriptures say was possessed of a "spirit of divination," was harassing them. Almost offhandedly, Paul confronts the spirit, and the slave woman is released and in her right mind (Acts 16:18).

The men who profited from her spiritual or mental illness are not amused. She was a source of income, as people threw coins at this raving psychic. In this story, Christ's messengers align themselves on the side of health and are opposed to those who oppress, dominate, and exploit this slave woman. The gift of healing that Paul and Silas received from Jesus is politically and economically dangerous. They have rocked the boat. So the merchants have Paul and Silas thrown into jail (without really knowing who they were or that Paul, for instance, is a Roman citizen and should have been exempt from such treatment). The story begins this way:

> About midnight Paul and Silas were praying and singing hymns to God, and the prisoners were listening to them. Suddenly there was an earthquake, so violent that the foundations of the prison were shaken; and immediately all the doors were opened and everyone's chains were unfastened. When the jailer woke up and saw the prison doors wide open, he drew his sword and was about to kill himself, since he supposed that the prisoners had escaped. But Paul shouted in a loud voice, "Do not harm yourself, for we are all here." The jailer called for lights, and, rushing in, he fell down trembling before Paul and Silas. Then he brought them outside and said, "Sirs, what must I do to be saved?" They answered, "Believe on the Lord Jesus, and you will be saved, you and your household." And the same hour of the night he took them and washed their wounds; then he and his entire family were baptized without delay. He brought them up into the house and set food before them; and he and his entire household rejoiced that he had become a believer in God. *Acts 16:25–34*

Later in the story, the magistrates discover that Paul and Silas are citizens and try to cover up their error. But Paul decides to rub their noses in it a bit. After stopping by Lydia's place to encourage the folks there, they head off again to share the Gospel.

There are some fascinating aspects to this story and to how we might use it to understand its relationship to the issues of sexuality and the church today.

Paul and Silas are singing hymns in jail. The other prisoners, it says, are listening to them—to these two *nuts,* perhaps. To others, they represent a tremendous sense of hope, strength, and peace that emanates from them. Paul and Silas are no strangers to suffering for the sake of the Gospel. They exuded joy in enduring suffering in the name of Jesus, for the sake of a slave girl, now free and in her right mind.

That same spirit I have seen among the South African political detainees, those who were tortured and illegally detained for years in prison for the sake of Jesus. I have seen it in those arrested in AIDS demonstrations, in those arrested in the early days of the civil rights movements, in antiwar protests. They have the joy of suffering for righteousness's sake.

For Paul and Silas, the earthquake was sudden and violent so that the foundations were shaken. The earthquake functions as an instrument of divine providence. One can only imagine how frightening that earthquake was nearly 2,000 years ago—no radio, no news coverage, no emergency preparedness. As the quake subsides, there is shock—a stillness.

The jailer, upon waking and realizing what has happened, simply assumes the worst—that his prisoners have escaped and that he will be killed for allowing them to do so. His fear of what his fate will be is so acute that he plans to kill himself. But, from the dark, there is a voice. How unbelievable that must have seemed to the jailer. The voice of hope, of mercy: "Do not harm yourself, for we are all here." The jailer is stunned, I presume, by this act of unmerited charity. The prisoners *free* the jailer from his death sentence! He gets his life back in those words from Paul. We never actually hear about the other prisoners again. But somehow Paul has managed to be the designated spokesperson and leader. On what basis did he convince the others to stay? Did the other prisoners associate the earthquake with the powerful presence of these hymn-singing religious folks? Better do what they tell you, and stay put!

The jailer's whole life and agenda get converted in this story. He no longer seems to care at all what the magistrates do to him. He takes Paul and Silas home with him, feeds them, washes their wounds, and is overjoyed to be associated with them through baptism in Christ. His whole life is turned upside down, and he is grateful! Now he is no longer a prisoner of his *old* life, but a free prisoner of Christ.

What a profound alternative reading, an alternative *earthquake theology* this is! Their own safety, comfort, or vindication is not an issue for them! Everything is about the opportunity to love, to be free, to testify, to save (the jailer's life and soul). There were no guarantees. The jailer could have chosen to kill the prisoners because he could no longer restrain them. He had the only weapon.

In some ways, the prison recalls the tomb of Jesus. I think of the angel announcing to the shocked visitors, "He is not here, he is risen." In almost a play on that story, Paul says, "We are all here." Of course the angel meant that Jesus was not there in the tomb. But the point was, Jesus was still *here*, but in a new way.

The violent earthquake (crucifixion, disaster) becomes the occasion for new life (Christ's resurrection, this jailer's physical salvation and spiritual conversion).

If, as the National Council of Churches of Christ says, it is true that the issue of homosexuality (sexuality, really) is a *huge seismic fault* that threatens to divide the Christian church, is this particular earthquake a disaster, an opportunity, or both?

I'm sure the visitors to the tomb that Easter morning at first saw the earthquake as perhaps *one more* disaster (on top of the crucifixion, perhaps another indicator of God's wrath). But instead, of course, it became the method by which the disciples came to know the miracle of the resurrection.

The church is having difficulty seeing the *opportunity* in this seismic debate on human and "homo" sexuality! In many ways, gay and lesbian Christians, imprisoned by the church's outdated and erroneous view about sexual morality, are like Paul and Silas. We might well be expected to use this "earthquake" (the conflict in the church over sexuality) to *escape*—to just pack up and leave. The foundations of the prison are shaking, for God's sake! Can the structures and theology of 2,000 years of Christendom really survive? Do we really want to risk being in the rubble?

But gay and lesbian Christians, like Paul and Silas, know that many non-believers are *also* imprisoned by the false theology of the church. The whole culture is permeated with the images and beliefs of a sexually repressed and phobic Christianity. Those who imprisoned Paul and Silas and the others were not the jailer but other more powerful forces "out there." There really was not any escape except to trust God, through their faithfulness, to convert the *entire system* from top to bottom. That's what Paul and Silas thought they were doing, and it is what we need to do!

So they start with the jailer, with the keeper of the tradition, the foot soldier of the power structure, who may have little power in the culture but who did what he was told. Who then are those good church people who keep believing and passing on traditions of condemnation, who are *just doing their jobs,* enforcing the outdated laws of the church? We can only hope and pray that we are faithful, like Paul and Silas, and *do not run away.* Will the experience of our testimony and our faith in God (not the church) be enough to convert the "jailer"? Because ultimately the "secret" will be discovered: that we, gay men and lesbians, are *citizens of the household of faith.* Just like the powers that have realized their error in treating the *citizens* Paul and Silas so rudely, someday the church will have to repent of its treatment of its gay and lesbian *citizens.*

There is also the fate of our *fellow prisoners* in the Christian moral theology jailhouse (tomb) that is both bankrupt *and* corrupt. Bankrupt because it ceases to bring hope, new life, or healing to men and women who suffer terribly not from their sexuality but from how the church *has made them feel or not feel about their embodied selves.* The *least* the church could do, one would hope, is to *do no harm.* But it does great, profound harm.

And I say corrupt. Many closeted gay and lesbian religious authorities harm others in order to protect themselves. They do so because they have what *they believe* to be "dirty secrets," shameful realities about their own sexual lives. Many in church leadership and hierarchies are sick with guilt, shame, and lying. Then they dump this on the rest of us. These are not *only* gays and lesbians but heterosexuals as well: all those who cannot tell the truth about their own sexual histories, lifestyles, or fantasies and who will persecute others who do!

Who are our "fellow prisoners"? They are people who say to me, nearly every day, "I'm not religious." This statement is a virtual political necessity in the gay and lesbian community. It might be okay or "cool" to be *spiritual*. But it should be a private, highly individual thing, like it used to be! Or very New Age or avant-garde. Never *religious*. Certainly not Christian.

When Fr. Malcom Boyd, Rabbi Denise Eger, and Rev. LaPaula Turner and I were arrested during an AIDS protest in front of the Los Angeles County Board of Supervisors, we were taken to our respective county facilities. The men had a much worse time of it than we did. They were chained to benches and not permitted to go to the bathroom for hours on end.

LaPaula, Denise, and I arrived just in time for lunch, which they served us in the holding cell. I think LaPaula and I were both aware that Denise was a little more of a novice at this than we were. I'd been in jail and had visited lots of people in this particular jail before. We sang songs for her and for ourselves (like Paul and Silas, I guess, though I didn't think of it at the time).

The guards were quiet and low-key, almost not seeing us. We were fingerprinted and kept in the smaller of the holding tanks. Across the aisle, separated by bars and glass, was the holding tank full of women, many of whom looked (to me) to be lesbian. I noticed that all of them pointed at LaPaula, Denise, and me. They saw my clergy collar. They were laughing, thinking this was cool: a bunch of preachers busted—for what?

I tried to communicate using the little sign language I knew. I smiled and joked, thinking they knew I was a lesbian. I was able to let them know we were there for an AIDS demonstration. They were all poking each other. They kept laughing until I looked at them and signed something like "I'll pray for you." One woman's face just clouded up, all angry. "Don't pray for me," she signed, folding her arms defiantly. Suddenly I realized that she thought I meant *praying for her because she was a sinner, a bad person, not like me.* This grieved and hurt me. No, no, I signed. "I'm a lesbian, like you." (I did look around before I said this to make sure no guards would see me.) "Really?" came the response, "No way!" She was all smiles again. "Then you *can* pray for me," she signed. Collar or no collar, I was a *sinner*, just like her.

We at MCC Los Angeles also found this story of Paul and Silas useful, especially in the face of hostile fundamentalist earthquake theologizing about the loss of our building. It became possible to see ourselves as those who could say, "We are still here," after the earthquake! We are not going anywhere; we are still being the people of God in Los Angeles, especially for the gay, lesbian, and bisexual communities, for people with AIDS, for *anyone* who feels judged or excluded from the people of God, especially because of their sexuality. We are still here.

Not arson, nor persecution, vandalism, or earthquakes can stop those who know the real truth: that we *are* citizens of God's wonderful realm whose ethic is one of unconditional love. We are still here, testifying to jailers, judges, magistrates, and our fellow prisoners. We do not experience things like earthquakes as God's special judgment or favor on anyone but simply as one more marvelous opportunity to share the good news of God's love and to practice that Way in our own city and neighborhood.

It is the Way of Christ that inspires us to see the Bible in this way. I believe that it is essential for gay men, lesbians, and bisexuals to take back the Bible. If we are not included among the stories and characters of the Bible, then it cannot be our book. It is also important for heterosexuals not to see the Bible monolithically either, but to see the people of the Bible as they must have been: as varied and complex in their sexuality as human beings are today.

8 • Angels at the Table

Throughout history and in many places in the world today, lesbian, gay, bisexual, and transgender people have been demonized, but Jesus is always turning the tables.

The passage in Matthew 19 about marriage, divorce, and eunuchs that was examined previously is related to another passage, Mark 12:18–27, in which Sadducees are trying to trick Jesus (again) with a question about marriage. I do wonder why he got asked a *lot* about marriage—because he was, presumably, single? Their question asks Jesus to comment on our future marital "states" in heaven. Jesus says people won't marry in heaven but will be *isangelos,* a Greek word meaning "equal to angels" (Mark 12:25). It sounds almost as if, once again, Jesus is not putting much spiritual significance on heterosexual marriage. Almost as if by *not* being married anymore we are *more* like angels. (Those who marry are contrasted to *eunuchs* in Matthew 19; then those who marry are contrasted to *angels* in Mark 12.) Were those who did not marry in this life *more* angelic to Jesus? Was he implying that angels are nonsexual or nongendered or that nonsexuality is *more* spiritual? This has been the prevailing interpretation—one that may have supported the idea of a celibate clergy and their spiritual "superiority."

Another possible interpretation might involve the fact that eunuchs and barren women were devalued in Jesus' culture (and other cultures). They were seen as "disabled," and this was a sign of God's disfavor. Marriage and children were the ticket to immortality, a sign of God's *favor.* Not to participate was to be "cut off." In another story, Jesus *also* questions the traditional view of physical disability as a sign of God's disfavor (the man born blind, John 9:1–34). I wonder if the connection between Mark 12 and Matthew 19 is that, in both of these passages, Jesus was challenging the devaluing and even demonization of those who did not have a heterosexual marriage and/or did not reproduce. Was Jesus indicating that being "married with children" was *not* the only way to please God? Was he covertly, subtly, validating the lives of those who did not fit neatly into that mold, and comparing them to angels?

It is useful here to remember a few other things. Jesus lived in a sex-segregated culture, where nonrelated men and women did not converse or socialize—a rule that he flagrantly violated. Jesus traveled with women, stayed in nonrelated, unmarried women's homes, taught and touched and conversed with women, including Gentile women. Friendship and even romance in this culture was largely a same-sex (if not erotic) activity. Romantic heterosexual love was the exception, not the rule. In that context, when Jesus spoke positively about heterosexual marriage and negatively about divorce, he did this in a way that honored women's needs and points of view.

Therefore, it is not so farfetched to see in these passages a critique of prejudice against eunuchs and barren women. Another way to look at the role played by eunuchs in the Bible is to compare it to the role played by angels. Eunuchs appear and disappear in scenes from the lives of major and minor biblical characters—especially prophets and kings. They are mysterious, androgynous figures who have specific functions: rescuing the prophets, carrying messages, shifting the balance of power, helping the underdog to win the day. This role sounds remarkably like the role of a *guardian angel*.

I also have wondered if the angels who appear in Bible stories seem *gay* in any way. What about the pair of angels who stopped to see Abraham on the way to Sodom and Gomorrah? Were they male angels or just male *appearing*? What if we were willing to view them as two *male* angels, a same-sex (or nonsexed?) pair that arrived at Lot's home and were subsequently threatened with rape?

What a difference it would make to see the *only potentially gay characters in the Sodom and Gomorrah story as the angels and not the wicked Sodomites!*

This would seem like an almost unbelievable reversal, especially with a demonized view of queer people. But in prisons in the United States and other countries today, for instance, it is *not* the lust-starved homosexuals who prey on poor heterosexual men and "sodomize" (violently anally rape) them. It is *heterosexual* men who prey on homosexual men or on smaller, younger, or weaker men (gay or straight), using them as a substitute sex object in prison. All prison officials know this, and police records substantiate it. In Los Angeles, they segregate gay men and transvestites into a separate city jail not because they are likely to be *predators* but *because they are likely to be victims* in the jail. I remember when I first learned of the segregation; I felt outraged. Then I learned from the inmates that segregation saved them a lot of suffering. In fact, some straight men *pretend* to be gay when entering the Los Angeles County jail system in order to do what they call "gay time" in the safer, homosexual jail. This becomes a problem for county jail officials, who once asked if MCC clergy would help them identify the *real* gays. Somehow they thought our gaydar (gay radar) would be foolproof. We know it never is. We declined to help.

This supports the alternative biblical interpretation of Genesis 19, in which the two angels could have been *gay* male angels who were the potential victims of anal rape. This interpretation actually *fits* with the sociological data about who is likely to be the victim or predator of male-on-male rape!

The two angels in Genesis 19 are performing a function that is consistent with that of both angels and eunuchs in the Bible: they are officials—messengers of God, attempting to protect God's people (Abraham and his family, especially Lot), shifting the balance of power, and rescuing the faithful.

These angels are coming to warn God's people and anyone who will listen about God's *rage*: God's rage at the violence, cruelty, indifference, and wickedness of these communities. The angels, in fact, just by their presence *provoke* and *expose* the very violence they have come to condemn. Gay and lesbian people do this all the time in our culture. These angels were nearly the victims of a hate crime!

While being themselves, fulfilling the purpose for which they had been created, minding their own business, they are nearly raped and killed by an angel-phobic, perhaps homophobic, crowd. Many gay and lesbian people are victims of violence every day just for minding their own business and going about their lives in the way God intended them to do.

I am not saying that all gay and lesbian people are angels or angelic. What I am trying to suggest is that there are powerful biblical correctives to the demonized view of gay men and lesbians—one of which, ironically, is Sodom and Gomorrah!

We gay, lesbian, bisexual, and transgender people need to see ourselves and be seen as *fully human,* neither as angels nor demons. I remember when we asked the World Council of Churches on behalf of MCC to *consider* including gay and lesbian people (who are executed and tortured in many countries just for being *suspected* of being gay) in their human rights agenda. We weren't asking them to support *civil rights* for gays and lesbians, or to offer some kind of religious validation. We just sought *human* rights: meaning the right not to be imprisoned, tortured, exiled, or murdered simply for being homosexual. When they hesitated, hemming and hawing, whining that this was "bad timing" for the WCC (never mind the "bad timing" for those being abused and murdered!), I realized the depth of the problem once again: they're not sure we're human! Human rights seemed to them to be an unreasonable request *at this time.* It made me remember that many people still see us as a "behavior" or an "issue" to debate, not as beings in need of safety or inclusion; Talking about human rights *and* gay and lesbian people in the same sentence was *difficult* for them to tolerate.

The humanity of "others" is foundational for understanding the essential obligation of hospitality in ancient nomadic desert cultures. In biblical times, if you traveled anywhere in the Near East, you had to depend on the kindness of strangers and acquaintances alike. You had to treat the sojourner well because you might need to depend on someone yourself in the future. There was a common appreciation of the true vulnerability, the fragility of life in a desert climate. *It was not a moral choice to be inhospitable.* To do so was to violate the deepest commitment to being human and in community.

This is one of the reasons the stories of Sodom and Gibeah are recorded in the Bible. These are stories about the abuse of strangers who required hospitality.

Sexual abuse of anyone—stranger, friend, or family member—is the grossest kind of inhospitality. Unfortunately, in our day sexual abuse is rampant. It is a sign of the deterioration of ethical human community. It is *not* primarily a "homosexual problem." It is a human problem. It results from the alienation from our own bodies and from the bodies of others.

Jesus came from a heritage of desert hospitality. As a person who during his ministry was without a permanent home of his own, he depended on the hospitality of others to survive.

Jesus knew what it was to give and receive hospitality. He knew how to be a guest. People were always inviting him to dinner! He rarely cooked; maybe that wasn't his gift! Perhaps others cooked for him because he knew how to appreciate good cooking. Also, he was probably a wonderful conversationalist. He brought interesting people with him to dinner and ate in all kinds of elaborate and humble settings. Dinner and table fellowship were always an excuse to talk about his passion—the nature of God and God's love, the way to live in harmony with neighbors.

He was vulnerable as a guest, dependent on the kindness of others for food and drink and presumably often a place to sleep, if not actually a bed. He probably had to deal with eating food that wasn't at its best and with accommodations that were less than adequate. He had to put up with attitudes—those who didn't like the men and women he chose to spend time with.

Sometimes he had a hard time setting boundaries. The dependence on others for food and drink and a place to sleep sometimes meant these people thought they could impose on him. How does someone without a room of his own ever have privacy? The Bible says Jesus went off to the mountains to pray or sometimes had friends or disciples row him across the lake. But even there he was often intruded upon.

But Jesus was not only a guest. He also provided his own kind of hospitality. He opened himself, his heart, his body. He invited people to question him, to touch him. And they did. He invited them to test him, to see if his words were matched by his deeds. He even invited them to challenge and criticize him, which they did.

The Last Supper is the only dinner at which it appears to me as if Jesus is really the host. He makes arrangements for this dinner with his friends and disciples. We have to assume that others actually cooked the food and served it, but Jesus has somehow arranged for this meal to occur. And the reinterpretation of the meal is a very powerful experience of bodily hospitality.

Jesus reinterprets the Passover for the disciples at this meal he is hosting. Jesus linked the story of the deliverance of the Jews from slavery to his own life and ministry and death. Jesus proposed a way for this new beloved community of Jews and Gentiles, slave and free, male and female, to embody freedom together, for the healing of the world. Furthermore, they are the guests of the savior. He is feeding them literally, as he has been feeding them spiritually all along. And he uses food and a meal to symbolize his relationship to them now and in the future. In fact, he asks them to think of him in the future whenever they share a meal together, whenever they eat bread and drink wine. Jesus' choice of symbols for himself is very provocative, sensual, and imbued with the images of hospitality.

Jesus asks his guests to ingest him, the reality of his life and death and teachings and being. He asks them to ingest his healing presence. This is a very risky image.

It certainly risks, at that time and at any time, being associated with cannibalism. But we do not feed on the dead body of Jesus at communion. We are invited to take him into ourselves, not as a dead martyr but as a risen, victorious savior. We are invited to eat and drink from the endless supply of the energy of God that was and is incarnated in the Body of Christ. This imagery is also very sexual, in a nonsexual context. It is sexual in a positive sense—it is about Jesus' own bodily hospitality toward us. The giving of himself physically, spiritually, and emotionally is connected to sexuality in the broadest sense of the word.

The fact that it has always been taboo to see *anything* in Jesus' life as sexual is a product of our distorted view of sexuality. If sexuality is a gift, then it is a gift Jesus had and experienced and shared. The longer I live and the more I heal from the sex phobia and sex obsession of our culture and religious culture, the more I see a desexed Jesus as a tragedy (sometimes a comic tragedy), if not a heresy. To imagine Jesus living to age 33 as a virgin with no sexual desires, longings, or experiences is utterly dehumanizing. I know and have been close to people who have chosen to be celibate. None of those persons has ever claimed that he or she had no sexual feelings, desires, or experiences.

It is as if sex is the *only* human experience we insist on denying Jesus—as if the "fullness of God" and human sexuality cannot cohabit in the person of Jesus or in any of us. As if we dare not explore that "enigmatic border" of the connection in Jesus of sexuality and spirituality. And this would explain why Christians, at least, dare not explore that connection in ourselves.

Only a Jesus vulnerable enough to be taken could give authentically. I think Jesus shared the gift of human sexuality in a poignant, sweet, metaphysical way at the Last Supper. He invited his followers into a permanent union with him, through bodily symbols of giving and taking. He was preparing for an ultimate act of hospitality—his own suffering and death for their sake, for God's sake, for the sake of the integrity of the mission. He was willing to open up his body and spirit to suffering and pain, to sacrifice, and to the possibilities of resurrection.

The process of creating friends from strangers is one of the most fundamental human experiences. Jesus talked again and again about how we might find ourselves in need someday, and wouldn't we want the stranger to behave as if they were our neighbor (the Good Samaritan—Luke 10:29-37). Jesus spent his life and ministry touching and being touched by strangers, some of whom loved him, followed him, cared for him, fed him, anointed him, and touched him deeply. Others in his life also betrayed and denied him, beat and crucified him. Some strangers refused his invitation, including one stranger whom it says Jesus *loved*. It is a strange thing to say that one *loves* a stranger, but it says that of Jesus. What did he love about that person? This was someone who had everything but was unsatisfied, longing for a deeper relationship with God. Did Jesus identify with this young man's search, his longing? Was it some mysterious sense of connection or communion in the moment?

I've been attracted to some strangers in my life. For various reasons, perhaps, Jesus was attracted to something in this man and called it love. But I've also even felt sometimes that I loved strangers. Sometimes when people come to communion at MCC, I have that experience. People whom I've *never* seen before, whose names I do not know, come to me for Holy Communion, to share the Body and Blood of Christ—the most intimate of all Christian sacraments. I don't know a thing about them or what draws them to the table or to this ritual.

Most of the time, if I don't recognize the people who come to communion, I'll ask them their names. I started doing this early on at MCC. I thought it was important, especially for gay and lesbian people, to hear their names at the communion rail. As they received the Body of Christ, to know that it was for *them* and that God and I wanted to know them. To know at least that someone calls their name in a sacred context. Sometimes someone may look especially troubled or needy, and I have asked that person if he or she needed a special prayer for some reason.

People come to the communion rail feeling extremely vulnerable, emotionally and spiritually. They trust that the persons serving know what they are doing, and will not only do them no harm but will minister to them. Sometimes they get more than they asked for; sometimes, I'm sure, they get less.

Communion with strangers is a very important part of our Sunday worship and daily church experience. I think about what it means for me to pray for strangers, to touch them, to feed them, sometimes to hug them, to say their names. And, more often than not, I find myself loving them with a love that is more than me. I know it is God's love loving them through me. This is a humbling and wonderful experience, as is having a stranger willing to accept that love from me.

It is also very sensual if not sexual, in the most innocent and non-exploitative way. We exchange bodily fluids at our communion rail—tears, sometimes perspiration, and the Blood of Christ. I have jokes with my congregation sometimes about how my vestments get a lot of wear and tear. By the end of the day, my vestments and sometimes my shirts and jackets have accumulated tears (and sometimes a little snot for good measure), sweat, makeup—as people have cried with me, laughed, touched, hugged, and kissed me, especially all day Sunday. Add to that the sticky fingers of children and, if we have a class, chalk dust, and I go home with a pile of laundry needing to be done. The experience is at once very holy, very tactile, and very demanding. It is a way in which I can provide bodily hospitality to strangers and friends, colleagues and family alike. It is a way in which I sometimes feel a profound solidarity with Jesus and with these strangers as well.

And sometimes the strangers themselves are angels. People show up all the time at the church who are probably mentally ill, lost, needy, not even caring what *kind* of church we are. Some of them are hard to deal with; very few are ever really dangerous. Some of them occasionally bring great gifts of all sorts. I've been prayed for in unbelievable ways by them. Some offer just a smile, or a perspective, or a joke. Sometimes I feel like they are themselves a test for me— especially when they show up on a bad day. Sometimes I feel like they are wasting my time and energy. But, when I really think about it, they are *not* the ones who have really wasted my time and energy.

Isn't the fear of strangers really the basis of racism and homophobia? They are based on fear of those who are different from us in some way. And, if we all start out as strangers, isn't the fear of strangers really the fear of intimacy, of getting close, of being vulnerable? Is this why we have

had to find ways to separate sexuality and intimacy? Are we so afraid
of our own longings and desires for connection, for closeness, that we
have developed a whole culture of fear for strangers? I believe that the
unhindered gospel that Jesus embodied calls us to overcome those fears.

If accepting that human sexuality is diverse and sacred constitutes a
"seismic fault" that is threatening to divide Christians and the Christian
church, how are Jesus' life, ministry, and teachings useful to us in either
easing the tension along the fault or practicing "earthquake preparedness"?

I believe that it is extremely difficult for modern people to understand how controversial Jesus was in his time and why. It seems clear
that 2,000 years of Christian teaching have put us to sleep with a "Jesus
meek and mild" so that we appear to be worshipping a *nice guy who finished
last*. The sharp and shocking message and practice that Jesus instituted
are lost in the layers of sentimentality. He has been co-opted and normal-
ized, especially by the majority and those in power.

It is useful to compare Jesus' Sabbath controversy with our controversy
about human sexuality. This analogy I *believe* will help us understand
Jesus' purpose and our dilemma.

What Exactly Was the Sabbath?

Many scholars have tried to discover ancient antecedents to the
Hebrew Sabbath. Essentially, the Sabbath was a weekly festival in which
Israel's relationship to God was honored and remembered. The Sabbath
was about rest. Tradition said that God had created the world in six days
and rested on the seventh. It was a celebration of creation itself. Israel was
to *imitate* God and honor God by resting on the Sabbath. It was a time for
worship and recreation.

The Sabbath was also connected to the experience of the Exodus.
Israel *could* rest because they were no longer slaves. Slaves had to work
seven days a week. But they had been delivered by a God who did not
believe they should be slaves to anything, including work. They were to
rest on the Sabbath as a sign of their freedom, as well as a sign of their
partnership with God in creation.

Over the centuries, the Sabbath grew in its significance. It began to
have political as well as religious meaning. "Keeping the Sabbath" became a primary sign of being a Jew. It was a sign of national identity.
Other nations were aware of this peculiar custom among the Jews. Nations

sometimes, in fact, used this information to gain an advantage over them. There are many stories in the Bible and the Apocrypha of Israel being attacked on the Sabbath. In some of these stories, God comes to their rescue. In other stories, Jews are martyred for their observation of the Sabbath. This becomes, by Jesus' time, a considerable historical legacy.

There were many in Jesus' time whose ancestors had died rather than defile the Sabbath. Keeping the Sabbath was an essential part of showing that you were a loyal Jew, that you were proud of your heritage, that you loved God, and that you were in touch with your history and your people. In addition, the Sabbath was already being mystified, as in the concept of the "Sabbath bride." In Jewish Sabbath worship, the Sabbath is welcomed into the synagogue as a bride into the bridal chamber. It is a lovely, embodied, holy, and sensuous image. The Sabbath is the bride of Israel, much as the church is the "bride of Christ" in the New Testament. There was a sense of a mystical union between the concept of the Sabbath and the concept of Jewishness.

Sabbath preparations could be simple or elaborate, as they may be today. The preparation and the celebration were a part of the holistic understanding of faith: faith includes one's heart, mind, body, and spirit. The Sabbath observance required participation of all of these in study, prayers, food, rest, family, and home.

The Sabbath provided a wonderful weekly reminder of the important things in a person's life. In our contemporary secularized culture, both the Jewish Sabbath and the Christian Sabbath are fading fast from the scene. We live in times of excesses, of 24-hour stores and restaurants, of workaholism, of slavery to work and profit, of the disappearance of leisure time. The days of regular mealtimes for families, of weekly play and recreation times, or of worshipping together are disappearing. Life's rhythms are very frenetic. For many people there is no Sabbath, no rest, no holy time of stopping to pray or relax, make love, or take time over a meal with friends.

Our modern Sabbath-free life is the nightmare the ancient rabbis feared. A society without rest is one without God, without health, and without balance.

The Sabbath was also the means of expression of identity. Not to keep the Sabbath is to forget who you are. Cultural and religious concepts of identity are located in the celebration of feasts, of holidays.

As much as my own ministry and MCC have been iconoclastic, we have also been about conceiving and creating culture, community, and traditions. And we do find that the hunger for roots and for tradition is so great even the very *new* practices get formalized quickly, and people get highly attached to them very quickly. So I have great sympathy for the rabbis and others who were alarmed by Jesus' Sabbath challenges.

Part of the problem in Jesus' time was a typical human problem. Sometimes those to whom we give authority go too far. Over the centuries, this had become the case with the Sabbath. Because the Sabbath was so important, many people were anxious to "do it right." So they asked the authorities to tell them in detail, over many centuries, what the proper way to observe the Sabbath was. What was the definition of "work"? How could I know for sure if I engaged in some activity that it was or was not work? As often happens with human beings, ordinary people gave away their own power and capacity to interpret for themselves the laws and word of God. And the religious experts and authorities, who love to spend time, energy, and breath debating the fine points of the tradition, had a great time with this.

Of course, what had been a fascinating philosophical debate for scholars, rabbis, and others became difficult, confusing, and overwhelming to laypeople who either went to extremes to be obedient or who began ignoring the experts (while sometimes feeling guilty). I want to say clearly that it is wrong—it is anti-Semitic—to see this as a Jewish issue. All humans in our religious and social traditions struggle with this tendency. Humans give away power to experts. Experts like to complicate things (that's sort of what they get paid for). Then the system gets too clogged and cumbersome, and there are rebellions and possibly reform. The idea that these struggles with the law are a uniquely Jewish issue is a mostly Christian slander of Judaism.

The idea that Judaism is about *law* and Christianity is about *grace* is a total misreading of the Torah and of the New Testament as well. The Exodus *is* about grace. The Hebrew prophets preached grace, and many modern Christians are so law-bound that they have, it seems, no connection to the divine grace that was Jesus' heritage and his passionate mission.

The other factor that affected observance of the Sabbath was that Israel had changed sociologically. The earliest memory of Sabbath observation happened among nomadic and then rural agricultural peoples.

Urbanization and political factors created a more complicated society in Jesus' time. People lived and worked differently from each other. There was a more complicated class structure. Some could afford to and did participate in all aspects of Jewish religious and cultural life. But there was also now a significant underclass, called "sinners," people who were no longer part of the mainstream. This underclass was created in part by years of urbanization and foreign domination. Alternative economics and foreign influence contributed to the erosion of national pride and identity and increased horizontal violence among Jews who had been conquered by the Romans. All these factors contributed to a sense that the Sabbath and Jewish traditions and life were really made only for *some*. For *good* people, for good Jews.

In addition, the reality that Jewish ancestors had died rather than violate Sabbath laws had had a certain kind of effect on the meaning of Sabbath observance. It became much more serious. It had become a litmus test of loyalty and "correctness." Its connection to joy, rest, recreation, leisure, and freedom from slavery was less important than its connection to loyalty to the law and national identity. The Sabbath, perhaps, had become weighted down, overloaded.

Into this picture steps Jesus, whom the Bible says "went to the synagogue on the Sabbath day, as was his custom" (Luke 4:16). Jesus had grown up hearing all the stories about the Sabbath and had observed the Sabbath all his life. Presumably, keeping the Sabbath was as much of an assumption in his household as in anyone else's. He himself was not a part of that growing underclass of people identified as "sinners" who no longer observed the Sabbath. He might have had ancestors in his own family who had died rather than defile the Sabbath of the Lord. Jesus never questioned the need for a Sabbath.

But what he did do was to flaunt his violation of specific Sabbath laws. I use the word *flaunt* deliberately. "Flaunt" is a very gay-connected word. When gays and lesbians are public in any way, even in the most modest and subtle ways, we are accustomed to being told that we are *flaunting* our sexuality. It is definitely an accusation with negative connotations. I'd like to redeem the concept and look at flaunting as a method of activism. Jesus did *act up*. He was protesting "Sabbath abuse," I believe. Jesus violated the Sabbath laws in a *public* way. He did not violate the Sabbath laws quietly, behind the scenes, discreetly, just because he thought they were unnecessary. He publicly and flagrantly violated them in ways that brought attention to himself, to his disciples, and to his teaching and ministry.

Also, Jesus violated the Sabbath laws not only to save lives or heal or for some *great cause*. He sometimes violated them casually, as in the story in Matthew 12:1–8. The disciples were walking through a grain field with Jesus and were plucking the ears of grain and eating them as they walked. They were observed doing this by the religious authorities. This was a clear violation of the Sabbath laws, and Jesus knew it. It was not an emergency. Every Jew knew that you were not to harvest on the Sabbath. Most reasonable, thoughtful Jews prepared their Sabbath food ahead of time, carrying it with them (they weren't allowed to walk too far either).

Obviously, Jesus and his followers had not bothered to prepare for the Sabbath. At this point, they were already perhaps "on the road," with no home base from which to prepare for the Sabbath. In any case, lack of preparation or consideration of Sabbath restrictions was like desecrating the memory of your ancestors. All this for a snack in the field? And, if they had simply acknowledged their error and stopped what they were doing, all would have been forgiven. After all, it was a minor infraction, really. It was nitpicking just a little. The problem was, Jesus was *not* sorry.

He *argues* about it. Even though he acknowledges that he is technically in the wrong, he argues (Matthew 12:3–8). He uses King David as an excuse, talking about how David ate the Bread of Presence in the sanctuary when he was being hunted down by the high priest and was starving and in danger. David thought that the preservation of life was, in that sense, above the law.

But Jesus was not starving, and, for the moment anyway, he was not in danger. In a way, I think he was being a smart-ass. He was in their faces about knowing the Scriptures as well as they did. He didn't buy that they had any more authority to decide what was proper on the Sabbath than he or his disciples did. This is what pisses them off. He talked back to them. He flaunted breaking the tradition that their ancestors had died for. He acted like he had more authority than they did.

Jesus doesn't stop there. He claims to be Lord of the Sabbath. Jesus acted like he thought he was God walking through that field with his disciples— embodying the love and rage of God. And along come the religious police. They encounter one who claims to be the Lord of the Sabbath, who is outraged because the Sabbath was supposed to be a gift.

It was a *gift of God to humanity*. It was not meant to be a burden, a drag. Maybe people were not *supposed* to die for it. The Sabbath was a gift. It was created so that human beings would not be crazed with work, would not enslave themselves to one another or to work or profit from business or even to do good deeds. It was created so that they would remember that they, as a part of creation, were good, and that pleasure, joy, rest, health, relationships, and relaxation were all part of what it means to live happily in union with God. God never intended for "religious police" to patrol the streets or grain fields in order to capture and punish the Sabbath violators. The *human* authorities were the ones who were violating the Sabbath with their tight-assed rigidity, anxiety, and narrow views of the Sabbath.

A sane, healthy institution of the Sabbath would not require intervention by religious police. The authorities were involved because something was not right with the institution. Wise, healthy Sabbath celebration was not so fragile an idea that it needed propping up by police. It would continue on its own merits, because it was a pleasure, because people looked forward to it. Jesus was, in that moment, the righteous fury of God. *God* was violating the human version of the Sabbath laws in and through Jesus and the disciples that day. It was a divine conspiracy.

And Jesus was touching and getting to know "those people"—those "sinners" who were not decent enough to follow the laws, to keep the Sabbath. They sought him out. He broke other laws by eating and drinking with them, by talking with them, and by touching them.

They were his Sabbath. With them, Jesus was at ease. They provided rest from the weariness of the battle. They were his joy, the balance in his days and nights. They were real, and open, and loved to hear (not debate) about the God Jesus told them about. They converted him every day with their need, their desire. The Sabbath was meant to be a *time-out* for everyone, the time when we took a breath, when we revisited who we are and why we do what we do. It offers a time-out from the games we play. Jesus' universalism went against his culture, as it does against most cultures when absolutized.

Jesus also went against the grain in his interpretation that the Sabbath was made for humanity. By Jesus' time, some were insisting that the Sabbath was only for Jews and that Gentiles who celebrated the Sabbath ought not to live.[84] Rabbis in the past had stated in the Talmud that "a Gentile who read the Torah was like a high priest." Jesus was definitely on their side. For many Jews, the Sabbath was a *national* symbol, a matter of cultural identity and integrity. A Sabbath for all seemed to violate that understanding. In a culture that was under fire, that was experiencing persecution at the hands of Gentiles, it must have seemed like betrayal for anyone to suggest that *all* people, including Gentiles, were eligible for the blessings of the Sabbath. In fact, Jesus' first sermon on the Sabbath in Nazareth, as recorded in Luke 4:16–30, starts out okay, but then Jesus manages to infuriate his listeners. He tells them that some of the Gentiles listened to the prophets better than the Jews did! He said this to people who were sick and tired of having to be nice to Gentiles who were oppressing them, taking their land and money, running their government. They didn't want to hear it, not from a local upstart who thought he knew everything. What did *he* know from Gentiles? They are so angry they chase him out of the synagogue and to the edge of a cliff. He has to sneak out of town and barely escapes.

The religious leaders of Jesus' day had forgotten that the Sabbath was meant to be an equalizer. Instead it had been co-opted into the service of class distinctions. It was meant to be an equalizer, a time when everyone, rich or poor, could rest and remember that, for all of them, freedom was costly and should be valued and cherished. It was also a *free* gift of grace, available to all, not just to some who could afford to "do it right." The Sabbath was also meant to be God's way of getting our attention. Instead, of course, people were paying attention to the rules about the Sabbath. I remember someone asking the question, "Which would you rather go to—heaven or a film and lecture about heaven?" People were choosing the latter. Not the Sabbath, but lectures and manuals about the Sabbath. The Sabbath was a taste of eternity, of life with the Creator. It was a holy time and space. It was meant to be a time of joy, pleasure, and restoration.

Jesus did not violate the laws of the Sabbath because he had more important things to do and the laws were in the way. He publicly flaunted the laws because restoration of the Sabbath was a *part* of his mission. If for Jesus the Sabbath was to be an *occasion of grace,* a means by which the people of God could regularly renew their covenant relationship, then for the "religious police" the Sabbath was the great litmus test of *sin,* of loyalty to nation and religious authority.

Like the Sabbath, sexuality is a gift from God! Although churches today might nod their collective heads at this basic theology of sexuality, they mean heterosexuality—or, as I have heard it labeled, *heteronorma-tivity.*[85] Let's face it, historically, sexuality was seen, at best, as a necessary evil—something humankind *has to do* if it is going to continue to exist. But it has also been seen as something degrading and base. The church, marriage, and Christian life were supposed to function like a *net* or *restraint* around human sexuality. Sexuality was to be controlled and policed (like the Sabbath). It was dangerous. Women embodied sexual lust, and men could easily become "prey" to its temptations. Sexism particularly poisoned our view of sexuality. Repression and obsession became the pattern we are still stuck with today.

I can imagine God's fury about this, at the way the story of Adam and Eve was distorted to mean that sex and the Fall are synonymous. The Sabbath, a gift of God, became a primary way Jews could break the law, committing sin. That is very similar to the way in which sexuality is rarely seen by Christians as a means of grace but as the primary occasion for sin.

We've ruined sexuality just like we've ruined the Sabbath. We've become obsessed with "doing it right," which does *not* mean relating sexually in ways that are mutually pleasurable, fulfilling, healthy, and balanced. "Doing it right" has often meant minimizing pleasure, an obsession with *what goes where*—seeing sexuality as a duty, as not being worthy in itself but only justified for the sake of reproduction. "Doing it right" has meant creating and obeying rules about when, with whom, how, how often, and what you were supposed to feel or not when you have sex. Religious police have haunted the bedrooms of Christians for 2,000 years.

"Doing it right" has certainly meant, just as it meant for the Sabbath in Jesus' time, taking the *fun* out of it. Maybe it isn't sex that aggravates the religious police—maybe it's fun. Like the Sabbath, sexuality was intended for our mutual joy and pleasure. Either as the means for procreation or as the most intimate, powerful human expression of connection and intimacy, *sexuality is about our being made in the image of God,* who is the Creator, and who is still creating. Insofar as we are in touch with our sexuality, we are connected to our passions, to our love for life, to joy and pleasure, and to the work of creation. The gift of sexuality is the gift of the means of *creative relationship,* of a God who loves joy, fun, and pleasure. What a thought!

Instead, of course, we have chosen to view and act as if our sexuality is a terrible burden—a curse, not a blessing—as a characteristic of humanness that needs to be controlled and legislated and about which we need to create endless rules and then enforce them with guilt and shame, with fines and jail sentences.

We have succeeded in so distorting human sexuality that healthy, whole, Godly human sexuality seems terribly remote, out of reach, the exception to the rule.

Sex has become something we both yearn for and dread. For many in our culture, dependency itself has become eroticized—so that sexual pleasure is derived primarily from the domination of others. Our sexual appetites and cues have been shaped and distorted by cultures that are sexist, racist, and homophobic and that abuse or hate children. Sexuality is seen as a *commodity*, something that is bought and sold, not shared. It is reduced by some to an addiction, masking the deeper hungers for intimacy, connection, love, and friendship.

On the Sabbath, the divine and the earthly were not to be polarized, but were to come together, to be married, to be in harmony. The Sabbath was the bride of Israel. Our sexuality is a gift from God. It is not meant to be something about which we are tormented and tortured, or with which we torture and torment others. It was meant to be one of the primary ways in which we experience connection with God and God's purpose in creation. Our sexuality, rightly lived and celebrated, is meant to draw us closer to God, not to drive us away from Eden. Millennialist theology claims that, in a renewed Eden, sexual happiness will be our portion. Sexuality is to be a joyful component of Eden, not what drives us away.

At one point in our stormy relationship, I teased the National Council of Churches of Christ in the U.S.A. by saying, "Do you know where I see the greatest unhappiness about sexuality in the world today? Not in the gay and lesbian community. Not in the prisons or hospitals I visit. Not even in the streets. The greatest unhappiness about sexuality I see is at *meetings of the National Council of Churches.*" And by that I meant that sometimes I felt as if MCC should have a counseling room at the meetings. Often we did, but it was my hotel room or the hotel rooms of other MCC visitors at the NCC. Sometimes we counseled in hallways or doorways. People would seek us out to talk about their gay son or daughter, their child with AIDS, or men who were gay but couldn't tell their wives. A heterosexually married staff person's partner died of AIDS, but he could tell no one. He sobbed in my arms in the corner of a meeting room. Men and women whose marriages were troubled for other reasons would choose *us* to talk to. I held governing board members in my arms who cried about their divorces or the struggles of being widowed. Some harbored shameful secrets or sought us out with painful questions. Some came to me wanting to know if I thought that so-and-so was gay.

Others knocked on our doors late at night, hoping to God that no one saw them. Some people would never be caught *dead* talking to me, not realizing that that in itself was a dead giveaway.

I could always tell who the gay or lesbian or bisexual people were at a conference with the "pamphlet test." We would put out our pamphlets on a table with other literature. People would glance at them; some would pick them up to peruse them, and some would take copies. But if the person saw our literature and *then looked furtively* over his or her shoulder ("Were any religious police lurking nearby?") before putting it down or taking it, I knew he or she was struggling with shame or guilt, and I knew he or she was probably gay or lesbian.

Some people were cruel and judgmental and asked inappropriate and prying questions they would never ask of a heterosexual person or wish to be asked themselves. There were people who knocked on our doors late at night looking for sex. Others came on to us at the dinner table, or *under* the dinner table, or sitting next to us on a bus on the way to an NCC event. Men who thought lesbian meant "hard to get" or that it meant we were bisexual or liked "three-ways" or that we were open to "kinky" sex. We who were supposed to be *worldly* and sophisticated about such matters found ourselves shocked at times, amused and sometimes not amused.

Some folks would proposition us for sex and then vote against us on the floor of National Council of Churches of Christ meetings. They were self-hating homosexuals, bisexuals, or heterosexuals experimenting while away from home. Sometimes the temptation to "out" these folks was nearly more than we could bear.

It also seemed to me that NCC meetings were, in general, very unsexy. They were dull, controlled, and often devoid of much passion. As young people, feminists, and social justice advocates faded from the scene, the meetings became even less "sexy."

I use the word sexy here literally—as in not many people acted like they were in touch with their own sexuality in a joyous way—and symbolically, as in *interesting* or *exciting!* It was as if *we* from MCC provided the "sexual energy" for the meeting. Late-night meetings, conferences at the hotel *bar* until two in the morning, confessions, intrigue, negotiations, capitulations, attempts at co-opting (seduction!), rage, grief, and feeling of any kind seemed mostly to happen in relationship to our presence. It was a way in which I sometimes personally felt exploited: It took years for me to understand this. We were their avenue for sexual projection and excitement. It was *not very good* for us, however!

Harassment aside, most of what we did at NCC meetings was to listen to people and to love them and try to keep our own boundaries, perspectives, and self-esteem. What sadness to witness all of this pain and struggle over the gift of sexuality! And then the National Council of Churches of Christ would continue to act terribly wounded that we were *forcing* them to deal with these controversial issues, as if it had nothing to do with them!

A group of Presbyterians, in the context of trying one more time to find a way to help the church work through its issues about gays and lesbians, suggested that the church needs a new basis for sexual ethics called *justice/love*.[86] The furor that this suggestion caused would make an excellent study in the sexual pathology of the church. But justice/love is exactly what Jesus was saying about the Sabbath. The Sabbath was made for us, not us for the Sabbath.

Sexuality is a gift for us; we were not created to serve an outdated, oppressive, sick sexual ethic. How can we, in the spirit of Jesus, restore and reform sexuality, as he attempted to do with the Sabbath? We can start by opening up to being playful and sexy.

Sex is supposed to be fun. Sometimes it is romantic and about passion and great love and all that. But whether with a new partner or with someone you've built a life with for 20 years, sex should be fun, at least sometimes. It can be lighthearted, casual, play for play's sake. And it shouldn't always be goal oriented (whether the goal is pregnancy or orgasms). Enjoy it! We can *learn* to enjoy what our bodies do and what they want to do just because we *can!* Good sex can be one wonderful way that adults play. It costs less than lots of other forms of entertainment. And you can be naked while you do it!

If we are honest, something about being naked is in itself plenty of reason to be playful. When we are naked, we are certainly vulnerable, and it probably makes us feel younger (as long as we don't look too closely). But even old people look like children in a way when they are naked. To be naked together when there is safety is to be free children together. Children love to take off their clothes—have you seen them? We laugh and think it is so cute when they do it. When we are undressing children to help them change clothes, they enjoy running from us, thrilled to be unencumbered, knowing somehow that doing this makes adults laugh and a little bit nervous. Children love to make us nervous and to make us laugh. They sense we have forgotten something, and they are determined to remind us.

Good sex is playful, at least part of the time. What if we could touch each other sexually the way children touch their own and other children's bodies, with a sense of wonder and discovery and laughter and trust?

Some of us are so weary, so worn, so tired of adult living. We need to rest *before* we can play. So we need the Sabbath in order really to have positive, playful sexuality. What if the concepts of the Sabbath and sexuality together are what could really make for justice and peace?

What if the church of Jesus Christ really saw as its mission to provide the Sabbath—rest for weary adults who overwork, rest for single mothers, for workaholic fathers, and overworked gays and lesbians? What if the church *stopped* overworking and really taught people to rest and play?

And what if the church was a place where people learned about play and the value of all kinds of recreation? What if we taught and practiced that sexuality is a form of adult play, whose boundaries and guidelines include justice and love? Maybe then our children would be happier to grow up.

The Sabbath must teach us something about justice and love. *All* were to rest on the Sabbath, even the servants and the sojourners within one's gates; anyone who came under the shelter of one's household was eligible and invited and expected to keep the Sabbath. In a society that enjoyed self-rule, this was no problem. In a society where Gentiles ruled or non-Jews were one's employers, this did not work as well. Often, poorer and more marginalized Jews under a system of foreign occupation were not in a position to bargain for the right to observe the Sabbath. In order to survive, to stay employed, they had to forgo this privilege.

Meanwhile, they were reminded by religious leaders (who were not in those circumstances) that their ancestors had sacrificed more than a job for the Sabbath—they had given their *lives*. They had done this, of course, not after generations of occupation but when the conquerors first came.

And they had done it together. There was not that same sense of cultural solidarity in Jesus' time. Many Jews had "sold out" in various ways to the Romans—the tax collectors being the most notorious. Because the Romans were less oppressive than other foreign governments (they allowed Jews to worship in the Temple, for instance), this process of becoming more divided over Sabbath observance had occurred very gradually, over time. Thus, the Sabbath that had been so unifying and universal in its origins, so available to everyone, and celebrated at so little cost, had become a source of division, pain, and inequality.

Jesus healed on the Sabbath. Interestingly, he did not heal people on the Sabbath only as a matter of life and death. There was a provision for that in the laws (there were all kinds of emergency provisions). But Jesus wanted to *normalize* healing on the Sabbath and to point out that it should not have to be an emergency, a matter of life and death. Any good done on the Sabbath should enhance the meaning and purpose of the Sabbath. So he healed a man with a withered hand, someone he could just as easily have healed the next day. He said in effect, "It's my Sabbath, and I'll heal if I want to." If the purpose of the Sabbath was to provide wholeness, balance, joy, and connectedness to God as a standard feature of one's life and week, then how was healing someone ever a violation of that understanding?

How is the gift of sexuality connected to healing? We certainly know that touch itself is healing. What if our sexual ethic were based on what *good* or *harm* sex accomplished, not on what rules we followed? Touch that happens in massage or by being stroked or petted, or by stroking or petting another (including a pet, for instance!) actually lowers our blood pressure and increases our mental and physical health! We all learned in science classes about the infants who were deprived of touch (while they were well fed and clothed and otherwise cared for). Touch deprivation caused a *failure to thrive,* which meant that some of them died. People are dying emotionally and spiritually, if not also physically, because they are not touched. Some people have learned ways to trade sexual "favors" for touch. This is tragic, sick, and sad. People should be able to have their touch and sexual needs met, together or independently, without having to trade, sell, manipulate, or be deprived.

I know that coming out as a lesbian and a sexual person was one of the most *healing* events in my life. It seems to me that that is true for many, if not most, gay and lesbian people. Contrary to what some have said, I do not believe that most gays and lesbians would prefer to be straight; we would *all* prefer to have the stigma removed from our sexuality, but I can recall meeting only a few gay men (and no lesbians that I can recall) who have wished they were heterosexual.

For some people, it is only the guilt and shame that precedes their coming out that are so painful. For some, the first sexual experience of any kind is overwhelming, frightening, and mixed with pleasure and pain. For most gay people to whom I have talked, their first *homosexual* experiences were confirming and included a sense of great relief, of coming home to their body—to their true feelings and nature. Sometimes the first sexual experience also included coming home to a new community. The strange thing is that, for many lesbians and gay men who came out without the benefit of MCC or good books to read or support networks, all the shame and guilt and secrets and even the hiding and lying were *worth it.* That amazing truth, in an awful way, attests to the power of authentic sexuality as healing.

My first sexual experience with another person was an experience of connecting the upper and lower halves of my body, of connecting sight and sound and smell and healing and touch. I was able to connect my hands to my heart, to my mouth and legs—all of me with all of me and all of her. I can still recall the incredible joy of the *permission* to touch and feel and explore. I became willing to be plugged in and turned on, and I found that everything worked! I felt successful; I who had felt so *disembodied* was pretty good at this, even the first time out!

And, of course, the sky was bluer, food tasted better, the songs were sweeter, the parting at college graduation sadder.

Don't you think that on the Sabbath, when the cares and distractions of work are not intruding, that the sky is bluer, the food tastes better, the wine is sweeter, friendships are more tender, and family is more precious? The Jewish Havdalah service has always been one of my favorite rituals. It is the service at the end of the Sabbath. Tradition says that you are to sniff from the spice box because, if you do *not,* you might faint because of the trauma of the Sabbath's departure! Tradition also says we get an extra soul on the Sabbath and that its departure will cause us to feel bereft and faint. The image of the Sabbath as a doubling of our soul—as, in a sense, a soul mate—is very sensual. The havdalah has the sweet, sad mood of saying good-bye to a lover—our lover, the Sabbath bride.

We need that time-out in which to reflect, to repent, and to ask the deepest questions about what we want the next millennium to offer our children and grandchildren. We can move toward a world in which no one would assume that a particular child is going to be heterosexual. Children would be aware early on that, whatever their orientation (whether they think of it as a discovery or a choice), their choice of partner or partners is not going to determine whether or not they have a right to live, breathe, feel, speak openly, or live with whom they choose. They will work in a profession they have prepared for, keep their children with them, have a right to survivor benefits, be on their spouse's insurance policy, and be buried with their loved ones. We will stop being an "other," outside of the normal considerations, always an intrusive *exception,* which is what makes us appear to be flaunting our sexuality. And we will never disappear again. Our silence is broken; we have found each other, our sacredness and God's amazing hospitality.

We are not going away. Not voluntarily and not at all. We are a necessary and essential part of creation and of every people and every culture. Sometimes honored, sometimes vilified, we are very often those who travel first to the enigmatic borders of cultures and millennia.

What if, in our new charter of human existence, we come to believe that all people have a right to a Sabbath, and a right to be who they are spiritually and sexually? And that all life forms deserve to be respected? What a powerful millennial vision! Fortunately or unfortunately, depending on your point of view, this is still a *queer* millennial vision. *But hold on, our time is coming.*

Appendix: The Roll Call of Eunuchs
In order of their appearance in the Bible

Hebrew Scriptures

GENESIS 37:36; 39:1—"Potiphar, one of Pharaoh's officials, the captain of the guard." This may be the same person mentioned in Gen. 41:45 and 46:20, who is described as an Egyptian priest. He was an "official" of the royal court who was also a priest, and might well have been a *eunuch*. Potiphar's wife tries to seduce Joseph (chapter 38), and the story makes a big deal of Joseph's repeated rejection of her. Does Potiphar's wife find herself attracted to *eunuchs* or those who might reject her? Does Joseph reject her only because he fears his master or because he is not interested?

GENESIS 41:8—The Pharaoh consults, in this verse, with "all the magicians of Egypt and all its wise men." Were these "shamans" who were also *eunuchs?*

1 KINGS 18:3—Obadiah is described as being "in charge of the palace" (the "palace master" is another term used, which in Daniel also translated as "prince of the *eunuchs*"). A parenthetical statement says, in the same verse, that "Obadiah took a hundred prophets, hid them fifty to a cave, and provided them with bread and water." He is yet another *eunuch* who saves the prophets of God.

1 KINGS 22:9—In this brief reference, the king of Israel summons a eunuch/officer (later referred to as a messenger) to locate a particular prophet.

2 KINGS 9:32–33—Two or three *eunuchs* throw the wicked Queen Jezebel out of the window to her death! They act as agents of God and the prophet Elijah.

2 KINGS 20:28 (repeated in *Isaiah* 39:7)—Isaiah prophesies to Hezekiah that Hezekiah's sons will be taken away to Babylon to become *eunuchs* of the king (of Assyria) as if this would be a shameful thing. Would it be a double embarrassment if it were not only a social/political disgrace, but also associated with being emasculated (either because of castration or homophobia)? Selfishly, Hezekiah ignores Isaiah, and apparently doesn't give a damn about the fate of his sons!

2 KINGS 18:17—"The king of Assyria sent the Tartan, the Rabsaris, and the Rabshaken with a great army from Lachish to King Hezekiah at Jerusalem." "Rabsaris" is probably a title, not a name, and it includes as its root the word for *eunuch,* "sari(s)."

EZRA 4:5 and 9:1—These are references to royal court officials, who function in these cases as lawyers and envoys, in the "go-between" role characteristic of *eunuchs.*

NEHEMIAH 1:1 to 7:5—Nehemiah, the great leader in Israel's return from exile, was a "palace servant,"—some say a eunuch—and the "cup bearer to the king of Persia." He sampled wine and poured it like a butler.

ESTHER 1:10–11—Seven *eunuchs* are sent to bring Queen Vashti to the king. They are among the few *eunuchs* actually named in the Bible: Mehuman, Biztha, Harbona, Bigtha, Abagtha, Zethar, and Carkas. What a parade that must have been!

ESTHER 1:13–14—This passage names the seven sages ("shamans," "wise men," or "privy counselors," also referred to in Ezra 7:14) of Persia and Media, who are also named: Carshena, Shethar, Admatha, Tarshish, Meres, Marsena, and Mecumen. They had "access to the king and sat first in the kingdom." Why seven *eunuchs* and seven sages? Are these magical numbers for this special caste of people? Are their names intoned in a certain formulaic way for a reason?

ESTHER 2:3—Mention is made there of Hegai, the king's *eunuch,* who is in charge of the women and their cosmetic treatments (Ancient Near East version of a hairdresser/cosmetologist). Eventually, Esther is put in his care (Esther 2:8). Hegai then advises her on how, as a new member of the harem, to win the king's favor (2:15).

ESTHER 2:14—Esther does really well, is "promoted," and moves up the ranks of the harem, where she comes into contact with Shaashaz, the king's *eunuch* who was in charge of the concubines.

ESTHER 2:21–23—This is the brief but sad story of two *eunuchs*, Bigthan and Teresh, who conspire to assassinate King Ahasuerus. But Mordecai and Esther foil their evil plot and are hanged (additional reference in Esther 6:2).

ESTHER 4:4—This verse refers to Esther's "maids and *eunuchs*," who are not specifically named.

ESTHER 4:5–11—This is the story of Hathach, one of the king's *eunuchs*, who serves as a messenger, a go-between for Esther and Mordecai. He's sort of like a palace spy.

ESTHER 6:4—*Eunuchs* accompany Haman to the fateful feast in which he is exposed as an enemy of the king.

ESTHER 7:9—*Eunuch* Harbona (mentioned earlier in the list in Esther 1:10) cleverly makes the suggestion (pure "poetic justice") that Haman be hung on the very gallows he had prepared for Mordecai. Oh my, don't mess with that queen (Harbona, not Esther)!

ESTHER 9:3—The officials, including "royal" officials, all become anxious to please the Jews because of Mordecai's great power and influence.

JEREMIAH 29:2—This verse refers to the queen mother and the court officials (saris, *eunuchs)* who are recipients of a letter Jeremiah writes to all the exiles.

JEREMIAH 36:11–20—This is the story of how the royal officials, several of whom are named, upon hearing Baruch's scroll of Jeremiah's prophetic writings, sense the possibility of danger and advise Baruch and Jeremiah to go into hiding, thus saving their lives. This is what *eunuchs* typically do in the Bible!

JEREMIAH 38:7–13—The story of Edeb-melech the Ethiopian, a *eunuch* in the king's house, is told here. Edeb-melech saves Jeremiah's life by pulling him out of the cistern, where he was imprisoned, awaiting certain death by hunger. Later, Edeb-melech receives an oracle from God, through Jeremiah, giving him assurances about his safety (Jeremiah 39:15–18).

JEREMIAH 41:16—*Eunuchs* are included in the list of categories of people who were captive but were freed by Johanan's forces: "soldiers, women, children, and *eunuchs*." They sound like, "men, women, children, and others" (referring to their servant status or sexuality status?).

JEREMIAH 53:25—Are the "seven men of the king's council" the same kinds of sages/wise men referred to in Esther 1:13–14? Is the "officer" a "royal official," a *eunuch?*

DANIEL 1:1–21—In the Oxford Annotated *NRSV*, this passage is labeled as "Daniel and his friends." Daniel 1:3 introduces Ashpenaz, called the "palace master" in the *NRSV*, or "the Prince of the *Eunuchs*" in the King James Version of the Bible. This kindly, older *eunuch* helps Daniel in a number of critical ways. In Daniel 1:11, the *NRSV* says that Ashpenaz offered Daniel his favor and compassion. The King James Version says Ashpenaz was "fond" of Daniel. Daniel and his Jewish friends are chosen by Ashpenaz to be trained as "royal pages," which might actually mean they are "eunuchs in training." Daniel and his friends excel in their training and are "ten times" better than the magicians and enchanters for Babylon (Daniel 1:20). Daniel excels at his "shamanistic" dreams and visions, which he, as a good Jew, interprets not magically, but as a gift from God.

The Jerusalem Bible describes the qualifications for the position of royal page to be "boys of royal or noble descent: they had to be without any physical defect, of good appearance, versed in every branch of wisdom, well-informed, discerning, suitable for service at the royal court"(Daniel 1:3). This is a good description of the qualification of eunuchs, I believe. The "handsome young boy" piece of this feels like "gay male sensibility" to me. People's appearance is commented on so seldom in the Bible that, when it is, it makes me wonder if the writer was gay.

DANIEL 2:1–11—This is the story of King Nebuchadnezzar's dreams, and of his woes with "magicians, enchanters, sorcerers, and Chaldeans" (Daniel 2:2). The Oxford Annotated *NRSV* says, "Chaldeans here means not an *ethnic* group, but a *caste* of wise men" (p. 1128 OT). It is interesting that a caste or class of people can be confused with an "ethnic" group. Was that because these wise ones, these *eunuchs*, were not just a professional class, but their role seemed more related to their identity? Did their identity select them for a particular role or profession?

DANIEL 2:12—Nebuchadnezzar orders all the "wise men" *(eunuchs)* to be destroyed, because they have failed to interpret his dream.

DANIEL 2:14–25—Arioch, a royal official (a *eunuch?),* also the chief executioner, helps Daniel out by giving him inside information. Daniel is very popular with these guys!

DANIEL 2:46–49—Daniel interprets the king's dream and is rewarded handsomely, including being made "chief prefect over all the wise men of Babylon." The "Merlin" of Babylon!

New Testament

MATTHEW 2:1–8—The wise men, called "magi," who were royal court astrologers, Zoroastrian priests, and *eunuchs!*

MATTHEW 19:10–12—Jesus offers a threefold typology of *eunuchs* in response to the disciples' questions about heterosexual divorce.

Jesus is a de facto *eunuch* in that the Bible and Christian tradition imply or state that he never married or had children.

ACTS 8:9–24—This is the story of Simon the Magician (the magi, a *eunuch?*) who attempts to buy the "magic" of Jesus' disciples.

ACTS 8:26–40—This story is about the apostle Philip's encounter with an Ethiopian *eunuch,* who is baptized a Christian by Philip. It follows right after the story of Simon the Magician. Are these a tale of two *eunuchs,* one a charlatan, one righteous?

Notes

1   Judy Grahn, *Another Mother Tongue* (Boston: Beacon Press, 1984), p. 6.

2   See Michael Cartwright, "Ideology and Interpretation of the Bible in the African-American Tradition," *Modern Theology* (April 1993).

3   The National Council of Churches, headquartered at 475 Riverside Drive, New York, was founded in 1950 and is the successor to the defunct Federal Council of Churches. In its heyday, it founded Church World Service, had a social activist reputation, and was a fairly progressive vanguard of the mainline churches in America, helping to fund, for example, Martin Luther King Jr.'s march on Washington in 1963.

4   Metropolitan Community Church (UFMCC) is a denomination founded in 1968 by Rev. Troy Perry with a special outreach to lesbians, gay men, and bisexuals but open to all people. For the story of MCC, read Rev. Troy Perry, *The Lord Is My Shepherd and He Knows I'm Gay* (Los Angeles: UFMCC Press, 1994) and Perry, *Don't Be Afraid Anymore* (New York: St. Martin's Press, 1990). See also Frank S. Mead, *The Handbook of Denominations,* new 9th ed., revised by Samuel Hill (Nashville, Tenn.: Abingdon Press, 1990), p. 167.

5   Originally the word was not *martyrs* but *heretics,* according to Rev. Jim Mitulski, pastor of MCC San Francisco.

6   Justo Gonzales, *Out of Every Tribe and Nation: Christian Theology at the Ethnic Roundtable* (Nashville, Tenn.: Abingdon Press, 1992).

7 Gonzales, *Out of Every Tribe*, p. 33.

8 Perry, *The Lord Is My Shepherd*, p. 201.

9 Martin Buber, *I and Thou* (New York: Scribners, 1970), p. 108.

10 Robert Goss, *Jesus Acted Up* (San Francisco: HarperSanFrancisco, 1993).

11 Phyllis Trible, *Texts of Terror* (Philadelphia: Fortress Press, 1984). Trible first used this phrase to denote Bible passages that described or justified violence toward women.

12 The "texts of terror" for gay and lesbian Christians are Genesis 19, Leviticus 18:22 and 20:13, Romans 1:26–27, 1 Corinthians 6:9, and 1 Timothy 1:10. See the MCC pamphlet by Rev. Donald Eastman, "Homosexuality and the Bible: Not a Sin, Not a Sickness," available from Church Services, 5300 Santa Monica Boulevard, #304, Los Angeles, CA 90029 (also included as "Appendix A" in Perry, *Don't Be Afraid Anymore*, pp. 338–46), and Jeff Miner and Tyler Connoley, *The Children Are Free*, p. 1–26.

13 John Shelby Spong, *Rescuing the Bible from Fundamentalism* (San Francisco: HarperSanFrancisco, 1991).

14 Virginia Mollenkott, *Sensuous Spirituality* (New York: Crossroads, 1992).

15 Mollenkott, *Sensuous Spirituality*, p. 167.

16 Elisabeth Schussler-Fiorenza, "Introduction," *In Memory of Her: A Feminist Theological Reconstruction of Christian Origins* (New York: Crossroads, 1983), p. xvi.

17 John Boswell, *Christianity, Social Tolerance, and Homosexuality: Gay People in Western Europe from the Beginning of the Christian Era to the Fourteenth Century* (Chicago: University of Chicago Press, 1980) and *Same-Sex Unions in Pre-Modern Europe* (New York: Villard Books, 1994).

18 Schussler-Fiorenza, *In Memory of Her*, p. 37.

19   Richard Hays, "Awaiting the Redemption of Your Bodies," *Sojourner Magazine* (July 1991): 20:17–21.

20   Michael Cartwright, "Ideology and the Interpretation of the Bible in the African-American Christian Tradition," *Modern Theology* (April 1993): 142.

21   Ibid.

22   James Cone, *The Spirituals and the Blues* (New York: Seabury Press, 1972).

23   Sirach 22:3, *New Oxford Annotated Bible,* Apoc., p. 115.

24   See Perry, "Appendix A: Helpful Reading," in *Don't Be Afraid Anymore,* pp. 344–45.

25   Bailey, D. S., *Homosexuality and Western Christian Tradition,* chap. 1, pp. 21–25 (New York: Longmans, Green, 1955).

26   *New Oxford Annotated Bible,* NRSV.

27   *Anchor Bible Dictionary,* vol. 6, pp. 99–103.

28   Ibid.

29   *New Oxford Annotated Bible,* p. 386, OT.

30   *Anchor Bible Dictionary,* vol. 5, pp. 816–30.

31   *Anchor Bible Dictionary,* vol. 5, p. 821.

32   *Anchor Bible Dictionary,* vol. 5, p. 1146.

33   *Anchor Bible Dictionary,* vol. 5, pp. 1145–46.

34   *New Oxford Annotated Bible,* p. 103, NT.

35   By the way, the *Anchor Bible Dictionary* is mistaken in this citation of the verse in Leviticus pertaining to homosexuality. It is 20:13, not 29:13. *I didn't even have to look it up!*

36   *New Oxford Annotated Bible,* p. 210, NT.

37   *New Oxford Annotated Bible,* p. 240, NT.

38 *The Expanded Vines Expository Dictionary of New Testament Words* (Minneapolis: Bethany House, 1984), p. 349.

39 Hays, "Awaiting the Redemption of Our Bodies."

40 Tom Horner compares these stories in the chapter, "The Men of Sodom and Gibeah," in *Jonathan Loved David*, pp. 47–58.

41 The chronology of the Sharon Bottoms case is as follows: In March 1993, Pamela Bottoms filed suit against her daughter, Sharon Bottoms, and her lesbian life-partner, April Wade, seeking custody of Sharon's child, Tyler. The mother's "immoral and illegal" lifestyle was cited as the reason. In September 1993, the child's grandmother won the case, though the decision was appealed. In June 1994, the Virginia Court of Appeals overturned the decision, prompting a counter-appeal from the grandmother. Tyler stayed with his grandmother during the appeals process. In April 1995, in a controversial 4-to-3 decision, the Virginia State Supreme Court supported the decision to remove Tyler from the custody of his mother. Again, the mother's lesbianism was cited as a reason for the decision. Despite the fact that Virginia's anti-sodomy law was declared unconstitutional in 2003 in the U.S. Supreme Court's decision in *Lawrence and Garner v. Texas*, the law is still on the books. Furthermore, in 2006, Virginia amended its constitution to take an even stronger anti-gay stand.

42 *Los Angeles Times*, Letters to the Editor, 22 September, 1993.

43 *Los Angeles Times*, Metro section 25 February, 1994.

44 *Los Angeles Times*, Metro section 25 February, 1994.

45 Phyllis Trible, *God and the Rhetoric of Human Sexuality* (Philadelphia: Fortress Press, 1978).

46 Gonzales, *Out of Every Tribe*, p. 25.

47 *Anchor Bible Dictionary*, vol. 3, p. 91.

48 Rev. Andy Braunston of MCC in East London wrote to me in 1992 of his corroboration of the theory that gays and eunuchs are linked in the ancient world: "When you were in London you gave a workshop for the three London churches and spoke of your interpretation of

the word eunuch. You mentioned that there was some scholarly debate on this. Over Christmas I came across a little pamphlet, *Hippolytus: A Text for Students.* In this translation the following is said in the section 'Of Crafts and Professions': 'A prostitute, a profligate, a eunuch or anyone else who does things of which it is a shame to speak, let them be rejected.'

The footnote explains that eunuch means male homosexual and, more importantly, quotes a French work by Botte (p. 37, note 7) [as] its authority for this. Even though Hippolytus is antigay it might be important that he uses the term eunuch in a way we would now understand to mean gay. This might help you with your work.

The texts Braunston consulted are G. J. Cumming, *Hippolytus: A Text for Students* (Bramcote, Nottingham, U.K.: Grove Books Ltd., NG9 3DS 1987), and B. Botte, 'A Propos de la tradition apostolique,' *Recherches de theologie ancienne et medievale 33* (1966)."

49 *Anchor Bible Dictionary,* vol. 2, p. 67.

50 Ibid.

51 *Anchor Bible Dictionary,* vol. 5, p. 87.

52 *New Oxford Annotated Bible,* p. 1020, OT.

53 Herbert Lockyer, *All the Men of the Bible* (Grand Rapids, Mich.: Zondervan Publishing House), p. 94.

54 Ibid.

55 *Anchor Bible Dictionary,* vol. 2, p. 667.

56 *New Oxford Annotated Bible,* p. 3, NT.

57 Mollenkott, "Appendix B," in *Sensuous Spirituality,* pp. 195–97.

58 William E. Phipp, *Was Jesus Married? The Distortion of Sexuality in the Christian Tradition* (San Francisco: Harper & Row, 1970).

59 *Anchor Bible Dictionary,* vol. 5, p. 422.

60 Hastings, *Greater Men and Women,* pp. 323–24.

61 Ibid.

62 John McKenzie, *Dictionary of the Bible* (Milwaukee, Wisc.: Bruce Publishing, 1965), p. 501.

63 *Who's Who in the Bible,* Ronald Brownrigg, ed., (New York: Bonanza Books, 1971), p. 257.

64 Vernard Eller, *The Name of the Beloved Disciple* (Grand Rapids, Mich.: W. B. Eerdman's Publishing, 1987).

65 Eller, *Beloved Disciple,* pp. 53-73.

66 Alexander White quoted in Lockyer, *All the Men,* p. 216.

67 *Anchor Bible Dictionary,* vol. 6, p. 573.

68 Tom Horner, *Jonathan Loved David: Homosexuality in Biblical Times* (Philadelphia: Westminster Press, 1978).

69 Horner, *Jonathan Loved David,* pp. 26–46.

70 *New Oxford Annotated Bible,* p. 366, OT.

71 Horner, *Jonathan Loved David,* pp. 40–46.

72 Mona West, "Ruth," in Watson Mills and Richard Wilson, eds., *Mercer Commentary on the Bible* (Mercer University Press, 1994).

73 Horner, *Jonathan Loved David,* p. 40.

74 Mary Hunt, *A Fierce Tenderness and A Feminist Theology of Friendship* (New York: Crossroads, 1991).

75 "Boston marriages" is a term from the Victorian era, used for women who lived together in lifelong committed friendships that were, it was assumed, devoid of sex. Maybe, maybe not! I remember hearing about "Miss So-and-So," who on her Boston tombstone had inscribed: "I haven't missed as much as you think!"

76 *Anchor Bible Dictionary,* vol. 4, p. 423.

77 Ibid.

78 Horner, *Jonathan Loved David,* p. 122. See also Miner and Connoley, *The Children Are Free.*

79   *Anchor Bible Dictionary,* vol. 6, pp. 66–68.

80   *New Oxford Annotated Bible,* p. 131, NT.

81   Mary Rose DiAngelo, "Women Partners in the New Testament," *Journal of Feminine Studies in Religion 6* (Spring 1990): 66–86.

82   Spong, *Rescuing the Bible from Fundamentalism.*

83   Grahn, *Another Mother Tongue,* pp. 6–8.

84   *Anchor Bible Dictionary,* vol. 5, p. 854.

85   I have Nathan Meckley to thank for teaching me this word!

86   *Presbyterians and Human Sexuality* (Louisville, Ky.: Office of the General Assembly, 1991).

my current Pastor. ☺

Subject Index

A

Adam and Eve, 82
African-American community, 40–45
After Auschwitz (Rubenstein), 12
alternative families, 97–98
angels, 139–141, 146

B

Bailey, D. S., 32, 52–53, 67
baptism, 62–63
barrenness, 85–87
beloved disciple, 105–107, 110
berdache, eunuchs and, 89
Bethany family, 104–105
The Bible
    author's early experiences, 25–28
    heterosexist biases of translation, 31
    influences, 19
    interpretations, gays and lesbians, 21
    love of, 24
    necessity of reading, 19
    objective reading, 21
    overratedness, 26
    ownership, 29
    relevance to gays and lesbians, 18–19
    storyline, 78
Biblephobia, 77–79
Bibles and Bulldaggers (Jackson), 121

blasphemy, 21
Boswell, John, 22

C

Camp Sister Spirit, 72–73
castrati, and eunuchs, 89–90
charismatic theology, 17–18
children, immortality and, 85
The Children are Free (Connoley and Miner), 32
Christianity, Social Tolerance and Homosexuality (Boswell), 22
The Church and the Homosexual (McNeill), 92
closet, slavery comparison, 43
coming out, God's truth and, 15
communion, 19–20, 144, 146
Cone, James, 42–43
Connoley, Tyler, 32
creation story, 82–83

D

David, 113–118
denominations, 79–80
disciples, 100–111
Don't Be Afraid Anymore (Perry), 80
double consciousness, 42–43

E

earthquakes, 129–138
eighth day of creation, 2

Eller, Vernard, 105–106
ethni, 81–82
eunuchs, 86–96, 140, 163–167
Euodia and Syntyche, 127
ex-gay movement, 35–36

F

family
    alternative families, 97–98
    Jesus', 98–112
    Jesus' redefinition, 39
    lesbian "sisters" and "cousins,"
      108–109
    Mary, Martha, and Lazarus, 108
    Mollenkott, Virginia, 97
    nuclear, invention, 97
    shirttail relatives, 108
feminism, 23, 26
Fiorenza, Elisabeth. See Schussler-
    Fiorenza, Elisabeth
forgiveness, 77
fundamentalism, 3–5, 35

G

gay centurion, 126–127
gender, continuum of, 83
gender confusion, texts of terror,
    64–65
*God and the Rhetoric of Human
    Sexuality* (Trible), 82
Gonzales, Justo, 12
Goss, Robert, 19
*The Greater Men and Women of the
    Bible* (Hastings), 104

H

Hastings, J. D., 104
Henson, Brenda and Wanda, 72–73
heresy, 21
hermeneutics
    feminist theological hermeneutics,
      23

    lesbian hermeneutic of suspicion,
      31–47
    new one of Sodom and Gomorrah
      story, 67–70
    queer hermeneutics, 3–4
    of suspicion, 31–47
    tribal biblical hermeneutics, 12
Holy Bible. See The Bible
homosexuality terminology, 58–61, 66
*Homosexuality and the Western
    Christian Tradition* (Bailey), 32, 67
hospitality, 70, 142–143
humanity of gay and lesbian people,
    141–143
humor, 15–18

I

identity, 11–13, 81–82
immortality, 84–85, 139–140
In Memory of Her (Schussler-
    Fiorenza), 22
infancy narratives, 95
inmates preyed on, 140–141
interregnum, 1–2, 3
irreverent humor, 16–17, 18

J

Jackson, Colette, 121
Jesus
    'coming out' as Messiah, 100
    disciples as family, 100–103
    family redefinition, 39
    hometown, 98, 100
    hospitality and, 142–144
    relationship with Joseph, 99
    on sexual sins, 111–112
    sexuality of, 111, 144–145
    women who challenged, 123–125
Jesus Acted Up (Goss), 19
Joel, Billy, "Just the Way You Are,"
    15–16

John Paul II (Pope), 36–39
Johnston, Jill, 14
Jonathan, 113–118

L

laughter in church, 17
Lazarus, 104–108
Lazarus Project, 107
lesbian hermeneutic of suspicion,
    31–47
lesbian invisibility, 61–62
lesbian "sisters" and "cousins," 108–109
lesbian spinsters, 110
Lesbos, 122–123
liberation theology, 20–21
The Lord is My Shepherd and He [sic]
    Knows I'm Gay, Troy Perry and, 13
Lydia, 121–123

M

magi, 95, 96
marriage, 40, 96–98, 139–140
Mary and Martha, 104–105, 108, 109
Mary Magdalene, 109–110
McNeill, John, 92
Metropolitan Community Churches
    (MCC), 5
    charismatic conference, 17–18
    deacons, 20
    denominations, 79–80
    formation, 80
    laughter in church, 17
    mission, 10
    NCC consultations, 32–33
    NCC relationship, 7
    New Orleans fire, 69–70
    as observer to NCC, 45–46
    Randall, Claire, and, 8
    Smith, Freda, 78
Middle Ages same-sex unions, 22
midrash, 77

Lazarus and, 107
Miner, Jeff, 32
minority groups, threat perception,
    75–76
misogyny, NSRV bible, 50
Mitylene, 122
Mollenkott, Virginia, 20–21, 97
murder, contradictions, 63

N

nakedness, freedom of, 158–159
The Name of the Beloved Disciple
    (Eller), 105–106
National Council of Churches of
    Christ (NCC), 5
    NRSV bible, 50
    sexuality and, 155–157
New Oxford Annotated Bible, 51–52
New Testament
    eunuchs, 167
    Scroggs, Robin, on male
        homosexual relationships, 11
    NRSV bible, 50–54

O

ordination of lesbian or gay people, 46
Out of Every Tribe and Nation
    (Gonzales), 12

P

Paul, 10–11, 127–128, 132–135
pederasty, Robin Scroggs, 11
Perry, Troy, 6–7, 13, 80
Peter and Cornelius, 80–82
Philo, sin of sodom, 67
play, sexuality and, 158
politics, 12–13, 31–32
prosperity as God's blessing, 85
purple, 122, 128

Q

queer biblical characters, 76–77

queer hermeneutics, 3–4
queer millennialists, 1, 3

R

racism, 40
  heterosexism and, 40–41
rape, Sodom and Gibeah *versus*
  Sodom and Gomorrah, 57–58,
  70–71
Revised Standard Version bible, 51
Rubenstein, Richard, 12
Ruth and Naomi, 38, 118–121

S

Sabbath, 147–161
same-sex couples, 113–138
Same-Sex Unions in Pre-Modern
  Europe (Boswell), 22
Saul, Jonathan, and David, 113–118
Schussler-Fiorenza, Elisabeth, 22, 23
Scroggs, Robin, 10
  NCC/MCC consultations, 33
  pederasty, 11
seismic theology, 129–131
Sensuous Spirituality (Mollenkott),
  20–21, 97
sexuality
  creation story and, 82–83
  Frymer-Kenskey, Tikva, on, 60–61
  as gift from God, 153–154
  image of God and, 154
  Jesus', 111, 144–145
  lesbian invisibility, 61–62
  NCC and, 155–157
  play and, 158
  ruin of, 154
shirttail relatives, 108
silence, 77
Sodom and Gibeah, 57–58, 71
Sodom and Gomorrah, 34, 49
  gay angels, 140–141

  inhospitality to strangers, 70
  Philo, 67
  treatment, 52–56
sodomite terminology, 64
sodomy terminology, 55
spinsters, 110
Spirituals and the Blues, The (Cone),
  42–43
Spong, John Shelby, on Paul's
  homosexuality, 127–128
strangers, 144–147
Suffering-Servant prophecy, 94, 96
Synoptic Gospels, Lazarus and, 105
Syro-Phoenician woman, 124

T

ten lost tribes, interregnum and, 2
texts of terror, 19, 35, 50–59, 64–65
Texts of Terror (Trible), 19, 49
theological anthropology, 4
traditional family values, 39, 96–97
transtribal tribe, 13–14
tribal biblical hermeneutics, 12
tribes, 2, 12–13, 81–85
Trible, Phyllis, 19, 49, 82
Tryphaena and Tryphosa, 127

V

Vines Expository Dictionary of New
  Testament Words, 66
violence, 73–74
  church teaching and, 34
  inmates preyed on, 140–141

W–Z

warrior lovers, 114
widowhood, 86
women who challenged Jesus,
  123–125
The Women's Bible, 32
World Council of Churches, human
  rights agenda, 142

Scripture Index

Genesis 9:20–27, 4
Genesis 10:6–11, 4
Genesis 19, 52
Genesis 19:5, 52–53
Genesis 19:5–8, 55
Genesis 30:1, 85

Exodus 20:13, 63

Leviticus 18:22, 63
Leviticus 20:2, 63
Leviticus 20:9, 63
Leviticus 20:10, 63
Leviticus 20:27, 63
Leviticus 21:17, 86
Leviticus 29:13, 61
Leviticus 20:13, 63

Numbers 16:31–34, 132

Deuteronomy 22:5, 61
Deuteronomy 23:1, 86

Judges 19:22–30, 57

Ruth 1:4, 118–119
Ruth 1:16–17, 38, 119
Ruth 4:14–17, 119

1 Samuel 10:1, 85

1 Samuel 16:4–23, 114
1 Samuel 18:1–4, 114, 115
1 Samuel 18–25, 114
1 Samuel 20:1–42, 115
1 Samuel 20:14–17, 115–116
1 Samuel 20:30–34, 114, 117
1 Samuel 20:35–42, 116
1 Samuel 20:41, 116

Psalms 2:4, 15
Psalms 113:9, 85
Psalms 127:3-5, 85
Psalms 128:3-6, 85

Ezekiel 16:46–58, 53–54

Isaiah 1:9, 53
Isaiah 53:7–8, 93
Isaiah 54:1–2, 4, 85–86
Isaiah 56, 90
Isaiah 56:4–5, 7–8, 86–87

Jeremiah 38:7–13, 89

Amos 1:1, 131

Zechariah 14:5, 131

Sirach 22:3, 50

Matthew 2, 95
Matthew 8:5-13, 126
Matthew 10:1-16, 57-58
Matthew 12:1-8, 151
Matthew 12:3-8, 151
Matthew 15:21-28, 124
Matthew 19:10-12, 91
Matthew 21:17, 104
Matthew 28:2, 132

Mark 2:1, 98
Mark 3:31, 100-101
Mark 3:31-35, 38-39
Mark 7:24-30, 124
Mark 7:27, 124
Mark 7:28, 125
Mark 7:29, 125
Mark 11:11-12, 104
Mark 12:18-27, 139
Mark 12:25, 139

Luke 2:49, 99
Luke 4:16, 150
Luke 4:21, 47
Luke 7:1-10, 126
Luke 8:1-3, 101
Luke 8-10, 125-126
Luke 8:40-48, 124
Luke 10:38, 105
Luke 16, 105
Luke 19:74, 104

John 2:5-11, 123
John 2:12, 100
John 4:7-44, 123
John 11, 104
John 12:10, 104

Acts 8:26-40, 92
Acts 10:15, 81
Acts 10:34-35, 80
Acts 10:35, 82
Acts 16, 132-133
Acts 16:11-15, 121-122
Acts 16:18, 133
Acts 16:25-34, 133
Acts 16:40, 122
Acts 28:31, 80

Romans 1:18-3:30, 59-60
Romans 1:18-27, 63
Romans 1:24, 26-28, 63
Romans 1:26-27, 64

1 Corinthians 6:9, 63, 64
1 Corinthians 6:9, 66
1 Corinthians 7:9, 128
1 Corinthians 9:5, 98
1 Corinthians 11:4-7, 64-65

Philippians 4:2, 127

1 Timothy 1:10, 64, 65
1 Timothy 3:12, 98

James 4:7, 18

Jude 7, 58